THE TITHE DILEMMA
EXPLORING THE BLESSINGS AND
CHALLENGES OF GIVING IN FAITH

AUTHENTIC SPRITUAL VALUES

Authentic Spiritual Values Group
authenticspiritualvalue@gmail.com

The Tithe Dilemma

Tagline

"Unlocking the Heart of Generosity: Navigating the Blessings and
Challenges of Faithful Giving."

Prayer

Heavenly Father, we humbly come before You, seeking Your divine wisdom and guidance in giving. You are the ultimate provider; everything we possess is a gracious gift from Your hand. We earnestly ask for Your assistance in nurturing generous hearts, devoid of fear or hesitation and brimming with the desire to honor You with all we have.

Lord, deepen our trust in You as we give—whether through tithes, offerings, or acts of service. Help us understand that giving is not about the quantity but rather about the love and faith we convey in returning to You a portion of what You have entrusted us. Let the joy of giving reflect our immense gratitude for Your boundless goodness and grace.

Father, we lift those who are grappling with financial hardships or uncertainties. We implore You to meet their needs and grant them peace. Reveal Your faithfulness to them and assure them that You will supply all their needs according to Your glorious riches. Strengthen their faith as they endeavor to honor You, even amid adversity, for it is in these moments that our faith is truly tested and strengthened.

Guide us all to embrace a lifestyle of generosity that surpasses the tithe. May we, as Your faithful servants, utilize our time, talents, and resources to bless others and advance Your kingdom. Grant us wisdom and discernment in our giving, and constantly remind us that giving is more blessed than receiving.

The Tithe Dilemma

May our giving draw us nearer to You, fortify our trust, and reflect Your love to the world around us. Bless every step of this faith journey and empower us to lead lives that bring glory to Your name.

In Jesus' name, we pray. Amen.

Blurb

"The Tithe Dilemma: Exploring the Blessings and Challenges of Giving in Faith"

"The Tithe Dilemma: Exploring the Blessings and Challenges of Giving in Faith" takes readers on a captivating and transformative journey to uncover the biblical foundations, spiritual insights, and real-life applications of tithing and giving. The book delves into whether the age-old practice of tithing still holds relevance for believers today and whether Christians should be bound by a specific percentage or embrace a broader, grace-filled understanding of generosity.

This book thoroughly examines Scripture, from the Old Testament principles of tithing to Jesus' teachings on the heart of giving, to explore the blessings and the challenges of living generously. Drawing from key biblical passages, such as Malachi 3:10, Matthew 23:23, and 2 Corinthians 9:7, readers will discover how giving, whether through tithes, offerings, or acts of service, reflects our faith and trust in God.

The Tithe Dilemma encourages believers to transcend mere obligation and embrace a life of joyful, purposeful giving. Whether you are questioning the importance of tithing or seeking guidance on how to give more faithfully, this book offers substantial, practical insights and unwavering spiritual support to help you live generously in faith, serving God and others with your time, talents, and resources.

This isn't merely a book about finances—it's a summons to live with open hearts and hands, join forces with God in His work, and uncover the delight of giving in faith.

Dedication

To all the faithful stewards who give generously, not out of obligation, but from hearts filled with gratitude and trust in God's provision.

To the pastors, leaders, and servants who, with unwavering dedication, guide and encourage the body of Christ to live in the fullness of generosity.

I thank my family and friends, who have shown me what it truly means to give sacrificially and with love, reflecting the grace and faithfulness of our Heavenly Father. Their selfless acts, such as standing with my family during the trial time., have been a constant source of inspiration for me.

May this book inspire you to live with open hearts and hands and a more profound commitment to serving God and others through your gifts and resources. I hope that you find this book beneficial and inspiring in your journey of faith and generosity.

Acknowledgments

I want to express my heartfelt gratitude to God, the ultimate source of all provision and grace, without whom this book would not have been possible. His guidance, wisdom, and faithfulness have been invaluable, and His Word inspires me. I am thankful for His lessons about generosity, trust, and faith, such as [specific lesson or experience].

I am also profoundly grateful to my family and friends for their unwavering support, love, and encouragement. Your lives have exemplified sacrificial giving, and I am thankful for each of you.

A special thank you to the pastors, mentors, and leaders who have shaped my understanding of stewardship and generosity. Your wisdom, teaching, and example have been invaluable in my spiritual journey and writing this book.

To the readers of this book, thank you for your interest in exploring what it means to live generously in faith. I hope this book not only encourages and challenges you but also inspires you to deepen your walk with God as you discover the blessings and joy that come from giving. Your journey through this book will inspire others and motivate them to live generously.

I want to thank everyone involved in this project - the editors, proofreaders, and individuals offering valuable feedback. Your dedication and insights have been instrumental in shaping this book, and I am sincerely thankful for your contributions. I hope this work will encourage others to live generously, not only with their finances but also with their time, talents, and hearts, all for the glory of God.

Author's Note

As I began writing "The Tithe Dilemma: Exploring the Blessings and Challenges of Giving in Faith," I was reminded that giving evokes mixed emotions in the Christian faith. Some approach it joyfully, seeing it as an opportunity to express their gratitude to God, while others grapple with questions of necessity, obligation, and the tension between legalism and grace.

This book is not meant to be the final word on tithing but rather an exploration of how we, as believers, can live generously in a way that honors God and reflects the heart of Christ. Whether you are grappling with the idea of tithing, have questions about its relevance today, or want to understand what the Bible says about giving, I hope this book will provide clarity, encouragement, and insight.

In my personal journey, I have learned that giving goes beyond mere financial transactions. It's a heartfelt proposition, an act of worship, and a deep expression of trust in God's provision. Through giving, we not only impact our own lives but also the lives of others as we participate in God's work.

As you delve into this book, I hope you approach the topics of tithing and generosity with an open heart. Let God lead you as you strive to honor Him with your resources, time, and talents. Ultimately, living generously is not just a command—it is about joining witted, reflecting His grace, and finding joy in giving through faith.

Thank you for accompanying me on this journey. May this book encourage you to embrace generosity in all aspects and live out your faith in ways that bring blessings to others and honor God.

Blessings

Foreword

Generosity is a fundamental pillar of the Christian faith. Throughout the earliest stories in Scripture, we witness a God who gives abundantly, provides for His people, and calls us to mirror His heart through our giving. However, the act of giving, particularly tithing, has often sparked debate, confusion, and occasional reluctance among believers.

In "The Tithe Dilemma: Exploring the Blessings and Challenges of Giving in Faith," the author skillfully navigates this important topic with insight, clarity, and grace. This book isn't just about unraveling the logistics of tithing; it's about grappling with the broader, more profound question: What does it truly mean to live generously as followers of Christ?

"I believe this book is quite timely. Our society often grapples with the conflict between materialism and consumerism on one hand, and the call to live sacrificially and generously on the other. The concept of the tithe, once considered a fundamental expression of faith and obedience, has sparked debate in modern Christian circles. Is it still relevant today? What is its role in the life of a believer under the New Covenant? And how can we give in a manner that honors God and reflects the heart of Jesus?

The author adeptly guides us through the historical, biblical, and spiritual aspects of tithing, offering a well-rounded exploration that draws from both the Old and New Testaments. More significantly, this book challenges us to move beyond mere obligation and embrace a giving lifestyle rooted in grace, love, and a deep desire to partner with God in His work.

In the following pages, you will discover insightful perspectives, real-life illustrations, and biblical principles designed to uplift and challenge you. Whether you are a dedicated tither or are just beginning to contemplate the concept, "The Tithe Dilemma" offers a fresh perspective on giving, infusing it with renewed purpose and joy.

The central message of this book is clear: Generosity extends beyond monetary gifts. It encompasses our time, talents, resources, and, most importantly, our hearts. My hope is that as you delve into these pages, you will be inspired to express your faith through radical generosity, confident that God will provide for every need as you give in faith.

I wholeheartedly endorse this book for anyone seeking a deeper understanding of biblical stewardship and the true essence of giving. The tithe dilemma may puzzle many, but as the author illustrates, the genuine solution is not found in rigid percentages, but in living a life wholly surrendered to God, trusting Him with all that we possess. I express my gratitude and anticipation for the profound impact this book will have on its readers.

Dr. Fasanya
RCCG Sufficient Grace Chapel
Indiana, USA

Preface

The topic of tithing has long sparked debate and reflection within the Christian community. For some, it is a deeply rooted tradition— a regular practice of giving 10% of their income as an act of obedience to God. For others, tithing raises questions: Is it a requirement for Christians today? How does it fit within the New Covenant? And perhaps most importantly, what does the Bible really say about how we are to give?

In The Tithe Dilemma: Exploring the Blessings and Challenges of Giving in Faith, I aim to dive deep into these questions. This book is not just about tithing as a practice; it's about understanding the heart of giving. The purpose is to explore how generosity, in its many forms, reflects the love, trust, and faithfulness that define our relationship with God.

Throughout this book, we will journey through Scripture, from the Old Testament laws regarding tithing to the New Testament's call for grace-filled generosity. My hope is that through this exploration, you will gain a deeper understanding of what it means to live generously—not just with your finances, but with your time, talents, and entire life.

Whether you've been tithing faithfully for years, are new to the practice, or find yourself uncertain about its relevance today, this book is for you. The tithe dilemma is more than a debate over a percentage; it's an opportunity to examine how we view giving as a reflection of our faith.

This book is meant to provide guidance, clarity, and encouragement as you seek to honor God with what He has entrusted to you. It is not a rigid rulebook, but rather an invitation to discover the blessings and joys that come with living a life of radical generosity.

As you read, I encourage you to approach the subject of giving with an open heart, seeking God's wisdom and direction. May this journey not only answer your questions but also inspire you to live generously in faith, trusting in God's provision and embracing His call to give from a place of love and gratitude.

Thank you for choosing to explore this important aspect of the Christian life with me. I pray that this book deepens your understanding of giving and draws you closer to God as you seek to serve Him with all that you are.

Blessings,

Authentic Spiritual Values.

Table of Contents

Prologue

In this book, we will explore the age-old debate surrounding tithing and giving, focusing on their biblical roots and relevance in today's world. We will address controversial topics concerning biblical text, unraveling the historical significance of tithing, and offering in the church and examining their contemporary implications. Join us on a journey to understand the motivating factors behind giving, drawing from both religious and psychological theories.

One compelling theory to consider in explaining tithing is cognitive *dissonance theory*. This theory suggests that believers, who are under financial stress and feel a strong religious obligation to tithe, may experience inner conflict. This discomfort can lead to a shift in their attitude toward money or a reaffirmation of their commitment to tithing, potentially deepening their faith in the positive outcomes of giving. Similarly, *B.F. Skinner's theory* suggests that behavior is influenced by its consequences, with positive and negative reinforcement shaping future actions. When individuals associate tithing with spiritual fulfillment, social validation, or financial prosperity, they are more likely to continue this practice.

Conversely, the fear of negative consequences (e.g., divine disfavor) might reinforce tithing. *Social identity theory* posits that individuals derive a sense of identity and self-worth from the groups to which they belong. Contributing to the group's norms and practices, such as tithing, not only strengthens this identity but also fosters a profound sense of belonging. Tithing can reinforce a believer's identity within a religious community, making them feel connected and part of a larger whole, participating in tithing by believers will affirm their membership in the group and their commitment to its shared values and beliefs, thereby strengthening the bonds of the community.

Utilitarianism, a moral philosophy that emphasizes the importance of actions that contribute to the overall happiness of the majority, provides a compelling perspective on the debate about tithing. It focuses on evaluating the morality of actions based on their outcomes. From a utilitarian perspective, tithing is justified if it leads to the greater good, such as supporting charitable causes, religious institutions, and community welfare. This philosophy underscores the positive impact of collective giving.

Deontological ethics, associated with Immanuel Kant, provides a philosophical perspective on the debate about tithing. It argues that actions are morally obligatory, permissible, or forbidden based on a set of rules rather than their consequences, but to duty and principles. Tithing is seen as a moral duty, particularly in religious contexts where it is commanded by scripture. It is considered inherently good because it fulfills a divine command, regardless of the outcomes or personal benefits.

Virtue ethics, rooted in Aristotelian philosophy, focuses on the individual's character and the development of virtuous habits. It suggests that moral behavior arises from cultivating virtues like generosity, courage, and justice. Tithing can be viewed as a practice that cultivates the virtue of generosity, helping individuals develop a habit that aligns with being good and virtuous, fostering moral growth and character development.

Social exchange theory posits that social behavior results from an exchange process aiming to maximize benefits and minimize costs. Tithing can be understood as a social exchange, where individuals give money to their religious community or church with the expectation of receiving spiritual benefits, social recognition, or divine favor, including intangible rewards like status, support, or spiritual growth.

Functionalism theory developed by Emile Durkheim, views society as a system of interconnected parts that work together to maintain stability and order. Institutions, including religion, play a crucial role in maintaining social cohesion. Tithing serves as a social function that supports the religious institution, enabling it to fulfill its roles, such as providing community services, social support, and religious education. This perspective highlights the importance of everyone's contribution to the community, making the audience feel the significance of their tithing.

Symbolic interactionism focuses on how individuals create and interpret the meanings of symbols and rituals in social interactions. *Tithing* symbolizes a believer's faith, devotion, and commitment to their religious community. The act of giving and the ritual associated with it carry significant symbolic meaning that reinforces an individual's religious identity and relationship with the divine.

Naturalistic theories highlight the biological, psychological, and social factors that provide valuable insights into the reasons behind human generosity. these theories help illustrate the inherent benefits of giving for individuals and society, suggesting that the advantages of fostering generosity far outweigh any potential drawbacks of withholding it.

According to evolutionary psychology, behaviors such as giving, and altruism have evolved because they were beneficial for our ancestors' survival and reproductive success. Giving, particularly when it involves aiding others within a community or group, likely played a role in establishing social bonds, strengthening group cohesion, and increasing the probability of mutual support in times of need. Key concepts within this framework include Kin Selection and Reciprocal Altruism. Kin Selection suggests that individuals are more inclined to assist those genetically related to them as it enhances the likelihood of their shared genes being passed on. Reciprocal altruism involves helping others with the expectation of receiving assistance in return, thus fostering a cooperative and supportive social environment.

Studies in neuroscience revealed that giving triggers the brain's reward system, particularly in areas associated with pleasure and satisfaction, such as the ventral striatum. When individuals engage in meaningful or selfless giving, they often experience a sense of euphoria or deep satisfaction, known as the "helper's high." Oxytocin, often called the "love hormone," plays a crucial role in social bonding and is associated with feelings of trust, empathy, and generosity. Acts of giving have been found to stimulate the release of oxytocin, enhancing the connection between the giver and the recipient.

According to Social Exchange Theory, human relationships are based on exchanging resources, with individuals aiming to maximize rewards and minimize costs. In the context of giving, this theory suggests that people are more likely to engage in acts of generosity when they perceive benefits, such as social approval, emotional satisfaction, or reciprocal support, to outweigh the costs. The theory emphasizes the significance of perceived fairness in interactions. When individuals feel their generosity is reciprocated or valued, they are likelier to continue giving.

Evolutionary psychology suggests that behaviors like altruism have evolved because they contributed to our ancestors' survival and reproductive success. When it involves aiding others within a community or group, giving may have been advantageous in establishing social bonds, enhancing group cohesion, and increasing the likelihood of mutual support in times of need.

Kin Selection and Reciprocal Altruism are two fundamental concepts within this framework. The kin selection suggests that individuals are more inclined to help those genetically related to them, as it increases the likelihood of their shared genes being passed on. Reciprocal altruism entails helping others with the expectation of receiving help in return, creating a cooperative and supportive social environment.

The theory of reciprocity emphasizes the significance of perceived fairness in social exchanges. When individuals feel their giving is acknowledged and reciprocated, they are likelier to continue engaging in generous behavior. Naturalistic theories, integrating biological, psychological, and social factors, provide valuable insights into the motivations behind human generosity. These theories delve into the intrinsic rewards of giving, both at the individual and societal levels. They also suggest that the benefits of nurturing generosity far surpass any potential costs or downsides associated with withholding acts of generosity.

Role of Believers in Tithes and Offerings

Believers are called to practice tithing and offering as acts of worship, acknowledgment of God's provision, and support for the ministry and those in need. While the Old Testament provides clear guidelines on *tithing (10%)* and specific offerings, the New Testament emphasizes the spirit of giving—*generosity, willingness, and cheerfulness*—over the specific amount or formula. In conclusion, both tithes and offerings play a significant role in the life of a believer as expressions of worship, support for ministry, and care for the community. The Bible encourages believers to give generously, sacrificially, and with a joyful heart.

Worship and Thanksgiving: Tithes and offerings are a form of worship and thanksgiving to God, acknowledging His provision and sovereignty (Deuteronomy 26:1-11, 2 Corinthians 9:11-12).

Support for Ministry: Tithes and offerings help support those in ministry, including pastors, missionaries, and other workers in the church (1 Corinthians 9:13-14, Galatians 6:6).

Aid to the Needy: Offerings support those in need, including people experiencing poverty, widows, orphans, and foreigners (Deuteronomy 14:28-29, Acts 4:34-35).

Expression of Faith and Trust in God: By giving, believers express their trust in God's provision and willingness to be stewards of His resources (Proverbs 3:9-10, Luke 6:38).

Tithing According to the Bible

Tithing involves giving one-tenth, or 10%, of one's income or produce to God. This practice is rooted in the Old Testament and is further developed in the New Testament. Under the Mosaic Law, tithing commanded the Israelites to give a tenth of their income, primarily agricultural produce, and livestock, the purpose was to support the *Levitical priesthood* and provide for those in need, serving as an act of *worship, obedience, and acknowledgment of God's provision.*

In the New Testament, while tithing is not mandated as a legal requirement for Christians, the principles of generous, cheerful, and sacrificial giving are upheld. The New Testament emphasizes the attitude of the heart and willingness to *support the work of the ministry and care for those in need, rather than a strict 10% requirement.*

In the Old Testament, tithing is well established. The concept of tithing is first introduced when Abram (later called Abraham) voluntarily gives a tenth of the spoils of war to Melchizedek, the king of Salem and priest of God Most High. This act, a voluntary gesture of reverence and acknowledgment of God's role in his victory (Genesis 14:18-20), sets a precedent for the voluntary nature of tithing. Abraham's grandson, Jacob, vows to give a tenth of everything God gives him if God protects him. This vow demonstrates Jacob's recognition of God's provision and commitment to honor God with his resources (Genesis 28:20-22).

The formal establishment of tithing is rooted in the Mosaic Law, as God commands the Israelites to give a tenth of their agricultural produce and livestock. The tithe is considered holy, belonging to the Lord, and set apart for God's purposes (Leviticus 27:30-32). The

Levites, the priestly tribe of Israel, played a crucial role in the distribution of the tithe. They received the tithe as their inheritance because they did not receive land like the other tribes. The Levites were responsible for the Tabernacle's service; later, the Temple and the tithe served as their means of sustenance (Numbers 18:21-24). The tithe expanded to include a command for the Israelites to bring their tithes to a central place of worship, such as the Tabernacle or Temple. Every third year, a special tithe, known as the "poor tithe," would be stored in the towns to support the Levites, foreigners, orphans, and widows (Deuteronomy 14:22-29).

Introduction

The Tithe Dilemma

Giving a portion of one's resources to a higher power or community, has been a longstanding practice deeply rooted in religious history and traditions. It has been visible in various faith and community traditions since the early days of human civilization, symbolizing both devotion and duty. Particularly prominent in the Judeo-Christian tradition, tithing has been a recurring theme in the Bible and continues to be a significant aspect of religious life for millions of believers today.

Despite its long history and deep religious significance, tithing remains a subject of considerable debate and dilemma for many modern Christians. In an era where financial landscapes have dramatically changed since the times of Abraham and Moses, questions arise about the relevance of tithing today. Believers grapple with understanding the blessings associated with tithing and sorting through any hidden challenges or misconceptions. Furthermore, they seek guidance on navigating the complexities of giving in faith while balancing their financial responsibilities.

The Tithe Dilemma: Exploring the Blessings and Challenges of Giving in Faith" seeks to address these questions by comprehensively exploring tithing. It aims to lead believers on a journey of true discovery of authenticity by shedding light on this ancient practice's spiritual and practical dimensions. The book offers readers a deeper understanding of tithing's significance, benefits, and challenges, providing a holistic perspective.

Understanding the Dilemma

The term "dilemma" refers to a situation where one must choose between two or more equally compelling options. Tithing presents believers with a choice: the Bible clearly emphasizes the importance of giving back to God and supporting the work of the ministry, promising abundant blessings for those who faithfully bring their tithes to the storehouse, as stated in Malachi 3:10. However, the complexities of modern life—such as economic pressures, financial uncertainty, and differing theological perspectives—can make the decision to tithe challenging for believers.

Some believers view tithing as a joyful act of worship and an expression of gratitude to God for His provision. Others see it as a burden, especially when financial resources are limited. The dilemma is further complicated by various interpretations of what tithing should entail in the context of the New Testament. Should it strictly adhere to ten percent of one's income, as prescribed in the Old Testament, or should it be more flexible, guided by generosity and grace? By considering these perspectives, believers can navigate the dilemma of tithing and make informed, constructive decisions.

The Purpose of This Book

The book The Tithe Dilemma avoids advocating for a one-size-fits-all approach to tithing, instead opting to explore multiple biblical, theological, psychological, philosophical, and sociological perspectives. This equips readers with the knowledge and insight needed to make informed decisions about their own practice of giving.

Furthermore, the book thoroughly investigates the historical origins of tithing, tracing its development from the patriarchs of the Old Testament through the Mosaic Law and into the teachings of Jesus Christ and the early Church. It highlights the blessings associated with tithing, such as spiritual growth, divine favor, and community support. Moreover, it does not shy away from addressing the challenges and questions that often accompany the practice of tithing, such as the necessity of tithes in the Church today, financial stewardship, and the appropriate way to use tithes based on Scripture.

In today's world, where financial pressures and the connection between faith and money can be strained, it is more important than ever for believers to grasp the principles of tithing. "The Tithe Dilemma: Exploring the Blessings and Challenges of Giving in Faith" is a valuable resource designed for individuals who are currently tithing, as well as those who may be questioning its relevance, facing financial dilemmas, or simply seeking a more profound comprehension of what it truly means to give in faith.

This resource caters to a broad audience, from seasoned believers who have faithfully practiced tithing for years to new Christians endeavoring to grasp the concept and anyone in between. "The Tithe Dilemma provides today's insights to facilitate the navigation of the complexities of giving in the contemporary world. It aims to offer a balanced and thoughtful examination that honors the diverse perspectives within the Christian community while staying true to the teachings of Scripture.

A Journey of Faith and Understanding

As described in the Bible and Biblical traditions, tithing extends beyond monetary contributions; it encompasses elements of faith, trust, and the sincere demonstration of belief. It reflects how believers perceive their resources about God and express their dedication to God's work. Tithing is a spiritual practice that encourages believers to trust God's provision, actively engage in their community, and revel in the joy of generosity.

As you embark on the journey through the pages of this book, I encourage you to approach the topic of tithing with an open mind and heart. Reflect on the teachings from the Bible, contemplate your personal experiences, and embrace the questions and challenges that arise. Whether this exploration leads to a reaffirmed commitment to tithing or a deeper understanding of generosity, the goal is to enrich your faith and nurture a stronger bond with God.

Far from being a mere 'dilemma,' tithing presents a profound spiritual opportunity. It invites us to explore the essence of living a life rooted in faith, generosity, and trust in the Provider of all things. It's not just about giving, but about the potential for spiritual growth that tithing offers.

Enjoy your reading.

Chapter 1

The Origin of Tithing: A Biblical Foundation

Understanding Giving

The notion of tithing is first addressed in the Bible in Genesis 14:18-20, when Abraham pays Melchizedek, the king of Salem and a priest of God Most High, a tenth of all the possessions he had regained in battle. Abraham's deed is interpreted as an acknowledgement of God's provision and bounty. In Genesis 28:20-22, Jacob promises to pay God ten percent of whatever he earns provided God protects him on his journey. This act was viewed as a vow and a kind of worship.

The Mosaic Law establishes the legal institution of tithing, in which God requires the Israelites to donate a tenth of their produce and cattle. This tribute is holy to the Lord and is to be given to the Levites, the priestly tribe who do not have land to inherit (Leviticus 27:30-32). The Levites inherited the tithe from the Israelites as payment for their service in the tent of meeting. This helped to fund religious rituals and Tabernacle maintenance (Numbers 18:21-24). Tithing is emphasized, with instructions for the Israelites to carry their tithes to a specific site of worship. Every three years, a special tithe shall be stored in the towns to maintain the Levites, foreigners, orphans, and widows (Deuteronomy 14:22–29).

In the Old Testament, God instructed Moses to gather free offerings from the Israelites to construct the Tabernacle. The offerings included various materials such as gold, silver, bronze, fine linen, and more (Exodus 25:1-7). Additionally, the Levitical law detailed various offerings, each with specific instructions and symbolic meanings. These offerings included burnt offerings, grain offerings, peace offerings, sin offerings, and guilt offerings, often representing atonement, thanksgiving, and worship (Leviticus 1-7). The prophet Malachi warned the Israelites, informing them they were robbing God by withholding tithes and offerings. He encouraged them to bring the whole tithe into the storehouse and promised abundant blessings from God if they did so (Malachi 3:8-12).

In the New Testament, Jesus criticizes the Pharisees for their meticulous tithing of herbs while neglecting the more important matters of the law, such as justice, mercy, and faithfulness. He acknowledges that tithing is good but should not be done at the expense of more significant moral responsibilities (Matthew 23:23). The book of Hebrews references the encounter between Abraham and Melchizedek, highlighting that Melchizedek, a type of Christ, received tithes from Abraham. This passage illustrates the superiority of Christ's priesthood over the Levitical priesthood (Hebrews 7:1-10).

Jesus praised a poor widow for contributing at the temple, saying she gave more than the rich because she gave from poverty, providing everything she had (Mark 12:41-44). Paul encouraged the Corinthian church to contribute abundantly and gladly, stating, "God loves a cheerful giver." He told them that God would supply abundantly, allowing them to be charitable at all times (2 Corinthians 9:6-8). Paul also acknowledged the gifts provided to him by the Philippian church, describing them as "a fragrant offering, an acceptable sacrifice, pleasing to God." This emphasized the idea of offerings as a form of worship and support for missionary activity (Philippians 4:18).

Tithes and Offering Perspective

The passage from Colossians 3:17 highlights the foundational principle that guides the approach of believers in every aspect of life, including financial giving. It underscores the idea that all our words and deeds should be carried out in the name of the Lord Jesus, accompanied by a spirit of gratitude towards God. This principle shapes our perspective on tithing and other forms of giving, emphasizing that giving should express worship and service to God. It encourages us to recognize the sacred nature of giving, to approach it with reverence and dedication, and to understand it as an opportunity to honor and glorify God.

The Continuations Perspective: Tithing as an Ongoing Practice is a viewpoint within Christianity that advocates for the continued practice of tithing as a relevant and necessary part of the faith. According to this perspective, believers are encouraged to tithe to honor God with their resources, following the biblical tradition of supporting ministry work and caring for the needy. This viewpoint emphasizes the idea of doing everything in the name of the Lord, with tithing being an integral part of that commitment. It sees tithing to support ministry work, highlighting its ongoing importance as a primary way to fund and sustain the work of the church and other Christian ministries, thereby emphasizing the significance and impact of their contributions.

The Discontinuation Perspective: Grace Giving in the Name of the Lord suggests that although tithing was a requirement under the Old Testament law, New Testament believers are encouraged to give without feeling constrained by legalistic rules. This perspective emphasizes the importance of giving freely and generously in response to the grace they have received. It encourages believers to provide out of gratitude and in the name of the Lord rather than because of obligation or compulsion, bringing a sense of joy and liberation in giving.

The Middle Ground: Tithing as a Guideline for Generous Living: This perspective regards tithing as a valuable initial step or principle for embodying a spirit of generosity rather than an absolute obligation. It encourages individuals of faith to consider tithing as a starting point for expressing the principles outlined in Colossians 3:17. This involves using tithing as a basis for engaging in additional acts of generosity and service, such as volunteering, helping the needy, or supporting charitable causes, in dedication to the Lord.

The Origin of Tithing

Tithing, which is offering one-tenth of one's income or produce to God or the community of faith, has long-standing historical and scriptural roots in the Judeo-Christian tradition. A detailed examination of the historical and biblical roots of tithing is required. It is critical to trace its origins to the oldest Bible patriarchs, such as Abraham, and its incorporation into the Mosaic Law. Furthermore, it is critical to investigate the unique situations in which tithing was implemented within the ancient Hebrew society and comprehend its importance in their religious and social lives.

Additionally, examining the critical biblical figures who practiced tithing, such as Jacob and the Levites, and understanding their contexts can provide valuable insights into the practice of tithing. By probing further into these specific contexts, we can gain a deeper understanding of the role and significance of tithing in the religious and social life of ancient Israel and its believers.

The Patriarchal Roots of Tithing

In the Bible, the practice of tithing is recorded to have originated in the era of the patriarchs, even before it was established as a commandment in the Mosaic Law. The earliest account of tithing is found in the story of Abram (later known as Abraham) and Melchizedek. This account is detailed in Genesis 14:18-20. In this passage, Melchizedek, a king and a priest of God Most High, brings out bread and wine to bless Abram after his victory in battle. Melchizedek praises Abram and acknowledges God as the one who delivered Abram's enemies into his hands. In response to this blessing, Abram generously gives Melchizedek a tenth of everything he has acquired. This encounter between Abram and Melchizedek is significant as it marks one of the earliest instances of tithing in the Bible.

The exchange between Abram and Melchizedek emphasizes the importance of tithe and how it should be paid. It exemplifies voluntary worship and gratitude, as well as a deep study on faith. Abram expresses appreciation to God for his victory by accepting Melchizedek as the Highest God's ambassador and presenting a tithe (one-tenth of his winnings). This generous gesture sets a precedent for worshiping God with one's money through tithing, establishing ten percent as a key part of biblical worship and devotion.

Jacob's Vow: A Personal Commitment to Tithe

"Then Jacob made a vow, saying, 'If God will be with me and will watch over me on this journey I am taking and will give me food to eat and clothes to wear so that I return safely to my father's household, then the Lord will be my God and this stone that I have set up as a pillar will be God's house, and of all that you give me I will give you a tenth". Genesis 28:20-22:

The biblical book of Genesis tells the intriguing story of Jacob, Abram's grandson. As Jacob flees from his brother Esau, he experiences a profound dream in which a ladder extends to the skies and angels ascend and descend it. During this visionary encounter, God repeats the promise He made with Abraham and Isaac, ensuring Jacob's protection and rewards. In response to this holy experience, Jacob makes a deeply personal vow to God, promising to give Him a tenth of all his future wages if He provides for him, stays with him, and safely returns him to his father's house.

This act of giving back also foreshadows the formalized practice of tithing that would later become an established part of the Mosaic Law. As the descendants of Abraham grew into a nation, God provided them with the Law through Moses at Mount Sinai. This comprehensive Law included instructions on various aspects of life, such as how the people were to live in the new land, how to worship God, and how to interact with one another. Additionally, God instituted tithing as a commandment, making it a regular and obligatory practice for the people of Israel. This further solidified the covenantal relationship between Jacob and God, emphasizing the enduring and weighty importance of tithing as a spiritual and communal obligation, uniting the people in their shared responsibility to God.

The Tithe as Holy to the Lord

***"A tithe of everything from the land, whether grain from the
soil or fruit from the trees, belongs to the Lord; it is holy to
the Lord. Whoever would redeem any of their tithe must add
a fifth of the value to it. Every tithe of the herd and flock—
every tenth animal that passes under the shepherd's rod—will
be holy to the Lord." Leviticus 27:30-32***

In Leviticus, God established the practice of tithing for the children
of Israel. The book defined tithe as ten percent of all agricultural
produce and livestock. It underlined that tithing was more than just
a voluntary donation; it was described as "holy to the Lord,"
implying that it should be set aside from one's earnings as belonging
to God. This commandment emphasized that everything the
Israelites owned was a gift from God, and that tithing was an act of
worship and recognition of His authority. The chapter also
discussed the redemption of the tithe. According to the Book of
Leviticus, those who wanted to keep a portion of their tithe might
do so by paying its worth plus an extra fifth. This provision allowed
for flexibility while still underscoring the tithe's sacredness.

Tithes for the Levites: Supporting the Priestly Tribe

***"I give to the Levites all the tithes in Israel as their
inheritance in return for the work they do while serving at the
tent of meeting. From now on the Israelites must not go near
the tent of meeting, or they will bear the consequences of
their sin and will die. It is the Levites who are to do the work
at the tent of meeting and bear the responsibility for any
offenses they commit against it. This is a lasting ordinance
for the generations to come. They will receive no inheritance
among the Israelites. Instead, I give to the Levites as their***

inheritance the tithes that the Israelites present as an offering to the Lord. That is why I said concerning them: 'They will have no inheritance among the Israelites". Numbers 18:21-24:

God particularly chose the descendants of Levi, one of Jacob's twelve sons, to serve as the priestly tribe within the community of Israel. In contrast to the other tribes, the Levites were not given a specific area of land when the Promised Land was divided among the Israelites. Instead, they were called to serve in the Tabernacle, and then the Temple. Their material needs were provided by the tithes paid by other Israelites.

The tithes were vital for the Levites as they did not possess land or other income sources. As per God's command, the other children of Israel were required to contribute a tenth of their produce and livestock to the Levites. This directive not only ensured the sustainability of the religious functions and rituals that were intrinsic to Israel's covenant relationship with God but also underscored the communal responsibility of supporting those wholly dedicated to spiritual service. The enduring significance of this principle is not just a historical fact but a call to action for religious communities. It reflects the ongoing responsibility to support individuals who devote themselves to spiritual service, making it an essential and timeless aspect of communal religious practice. This principle reminds us of the importance of our role in sustaining the spiritual fabric of our communities.

Tithing for the Poor: A Social and Religious Responsibility

"Be sure to set aside a tenth of all that your fields produce each year. Eat the tithe of your grain, new wine and olive oil, and the firstborn of your herds and flocks in the presence of the Lord your God at the place he will choose as a dwelling for his Name, so that you may learn to revere the Lord your God always. But if that place is too distant and you have been blessed by the Lord your God and cannot carry your tithe (because the place where the Lord will choose to put his Name is so far away), then exchange your tithe for silver, and take the silver with you and go to the place the Lord your God will choose. Use the silver to buy whatever you like: cattle, sheep, wine or other fermented drink, or anything you wish. Then you and your household shall eat there in the presence of the Lord your God and rejoice. And do not neglect the Levites living in your towns, for they have no allotment or inheritance of their own. At the end of every three years, bring all the tithes of that year's produce and store it in your towns, so that the Levites (who have no allotment or inheritance of their own) and the foreigners, the fatherless and the widows who live in your towns may come and eat and be satisfied, and so that the Lord your God may bless you in all the work of your hands." Deuteronomy 14:22-29.

The book of Deuteronomy gives detailed instructions on tithing, emphasizing its communal nature and importance in displaying regard for God and thanks for His favors. The Israelites were instructed to set aside a tenth of their harvest for a community supper at the designated place of worship, either the Tabernacle or the Temple. This practice, which has persisted in many Jewish communities, is a physical way to celebrate and appreciate God's provision. The scripture highlights the significance of tithing to support society's most vulnerable people. Every third year, a special tithe would be allocated in the towns to benefit the Levites, foreigners, orphans, and widows. This fulfilled a religious obligation and served as a form of social welfare, ensuring that those in need were cared for. By integrating this command into the law, the practice of tithing was not only a religious duty but also a moral obligation to promote justice and compassion within the community.

Tithing as a Foundational Practice

The Bible depicts tithing as a fundamental practice that intertwines faith, worship, and communal responsibility. Through the historical accounts of Abram and Jacob and its establishment in the Mosaic Law, tithing emerges as a crucial element of the covenant relationship between God and humanity. It was implemented as a way for the people of God to recognize His sovereignty and provision. Giving a tenth of their resources, the Israelites demonstrated their trust in God as the ultimate provider and expressed gratitude for His blessings. Tithing was not solely an economic transaction but a spiritual act reinforcing the bond between God and His people.

Furthermore, tithing played a pivotal role in supporting Israel's religious infrastructure. The Levites, tasked with maintaining the Tabernacle and later the Temple, relied on the tithes for their sustenance. Without this system of support, the nation's religious life would have been unsustainable. Tithing, therefore, ensured the continuity of worship, sacrifices, and other religious practices, thereby upholding the community's spiritual well-being.

According to the Mosaic Law, the concept of tithing held significant social importance, as a portion of the tithe was dedicated to supporting people experiencing poverty, fatherlessness, and widows. This demonstrated the integration of social justice into Israelite society. Tithing served as a way for the community to collectively fulfill its responsibility towards the vulnerable, reflecting the character of God, who is described as a protector of the needy.

As we progress through this book, we'll look at how the ideas of tithing established in the Old Testament continue to impact Christian thought and practice today. While the specifics of the tithe may have changed, the underlying values of worship, faith in God, support for ministry, and caring for the poor are as relevant today as they were in ancient Israel.

It is crucial to remember that tithing is more than just a historical tradition; it is a fundamental principle that has shaped how Christians view their connection with God, their responsibilities to one another, and their attitude toward worldly prosperity. Understanding the origins of tithing helps believers appreciate its long-term relevance and encourages us to examine how we might properly follow and apply these principles in our lives.

Chapter 2

Tithing in the Law of Moses: Commandments and Purpose

The Old Testament Bible promotes tithing as a voluntary act of worship and an important part of a believer's life. The Mosaic Law provides specific guidance on the purpose of tithing, emphasizing its importance as a component of the community's spiritual and social framework. Our examination of the Mosaic Law's tithing commandments will focus understanding its principal goals, which include supporting the priesthood, providing for those in need, and encouraging communal worship. Furthermore, we will analyze the function of tithing in Israel's spiritual and social life, using biblical teachings to effectively demonstrate our ideas.

Tithing as a Commandment: A Sacred Obligation

Tithing evolved from a voluntary practice observed by the patriarchs to a sacred obligation for the people of Israel. This transition signified the significance of tithing as not just a mere tradition but an essential act of obedience and devotion to God. It demonstrated a commitment to honoring God with the first fruits of one's labor and resources. This sacred obligation served as a tangible expression of the people's faith and trust in God's provision and sovereignty.

Tithes and Offerings: Holy to the Lord

"A tithe of everything from the land, whether grain from the soil or fruit from the trees, belongs to the Lord; it is holy to the Lord. Whoever would redeem any of their tithe must add

> *a fifth of the value to it. Every tithe of the herd and flock—*
> *every tenth animal that passes under the shepherd's rod—will*
> *be holy to the Lord. No one may pick out the good from the*
> *bad or make any substitution. If anyone does make a*
> *substitution, both the animal and its substitute become holy*
> *and cannot be redeemed." Leviticus 27:30-34.*

According to the book of Leviticus, offering a tenth of one's agricultural produce to the Lord is "holy to the Lord." This notion of holiness implies that the tithe was to be laid aside solely for God. At the period, agriculture was the Israelites' principal source of revenue, so the tithe was a broad commandment that applied to many facets of life. Due to its sacred character, the tithe could not be utilized for any other purpose. If the Israelites wanted to redeem a portion of their tithe for personal use, they may do so, but they had to pay the amount plus an additional fifth. This law protected the holiness of the tithe and God's portion.

Leviticus emphasizes the importance of tithing and specifies that it should not be given selectively. The Israelites were prohibited from substituting lower-quality produce or animals for the tithe. They were commanded to give every tenth animal and a tenth of the produce to the Lord, regardless of its quality. This rule reinforced the principle that tithing is about honoring God with the first and best of what one has. It reflects a heart of true worship and reverence for God.

The Purposes of Tithing in the Mosaic Law

Believers often question the importance of tithing and its significance, significantly when the funds may not benefit God directly. However, the reasons for tithing were deeply examined and elucidated in the Mosaic Law. Each purpose played a vital role in the lives of the Israelites, fostering a sense of unity and belonging within the community. It is crucial to understand that tithing is not just a religious duty; it also upholds social norms, ensuring that the community of faith operates according to God's commands and plans, reflecting his character. Moreover, tithing serves various purposes, including supporting the priesthood and providing for the community's needs.

Supporting the Priesthood: In the Old Testament, the concept of tithing was closely linked to supporting the Levites, who were part of the priestly tribe of Israel. The Levites were dedicated to serving in religious duties and were not given a specific portion of land like the other tribes of Israel. Instead of land, the Lord was their inheritance. To ensure that the Levites were provided for, God commanded the other tribes of Israel to give a tenth of their earnings as tithes and offerings to support the Levites in their service and daily lives. This practice of tithing was meant to sustain and care for the spiritual leaders and support the religious community of the Levites.

"I give to the Levites all the tithes in Israel as their inheritance in return for the work they do while serving at the tent of meeting. From now on the Israelites must not go near the tent of meeting, or they will bear the consequences of their sin and will die. It is the Levites who are to do the work at the tent of

meeting and bear the responsibility for any offenses they commit against it. This is a lasting ordinance for the generations to come. They will receive no inheritance among the Israelites. Instead, I give to the Levites as their inheritance the tithes that the Israelites present as an offering to the Lord. That is why I said concerning them: 'They will have no inheritance among the Israelites". Numbers 18:21-24

Tithing to the Levites served as both a religious obligation and a practical means to support the spiritual leadership within Israel. It provided the Levites with the necessary resources to entirely focus on their sacred responsibilities without the burden of having to earn a living through agriculture or other means. This allowed them to dedicate themselves to leading religious rituals, maintaining the Tabernacle (the Temple), and imparting knowledge of the Laws to the people.

By instructing the Israelites to contribute a tenth of their produce to the Levites, God ensured the continuity of Israel's spiritual life and the undivided commitment of the Levites to their sacred duties

Providing for the Needy: In the Mosaic Law, believers were required to give a tenth of their income to support and provide for the poor and needy within their community. The law emphasized the importance of social justice and caring for the vulnerable. These values were deeply ingrained in the practice of tithing among the children of Israel, reflecting a strong sense of communal responsibility and support for those in need.

"At the end of every three years, bring all the tithes of that year's produce and store it in your towns, so that the Levites

(who have no allotment or inheritance of their own) and the foreigners, the fatherless and the widows who live in your towns may come and eat and be satisfied, and so that the Lord your God may bless you in all the work of your hands.".
Deuteronomy 14:28-29

God commanded the Israelites to set aside a special tithe every third year, referred to as the "poor tithe," and store it in the storehouse. This tithe was explicitly designated for the Levites, foreigners, orphans, and widows, who were among the most vulnerable members of society, often without the means to support themselves. The purpose of this tithe was to serve as a safety net to meet their basic needs.

The Mosaic Law underscored the social aspect of tithing, emphasizing that it was not only a religious duty but also an expression of communal responsibility and compassion. This included caring for needy people, highlighting that worship was inseparable from justice and mercy toward others. Furthermore, there were two-fold blessings associated with the practice of tithing. Firstly, it ensured that the community's most vulnerable members were cared for, reflecting God's heart for justice and compassion. Secondly, the doctrine of tithing was a blessing to the givers, reflecting their obedience to God's commands and opening the way for His continued favor and provision in their lives.

Promoting Communal Worship: Tithing was a fundamental practice in the religious life of the Israelites, playing a significant role in fostering communal worship and solidarity within the community. According to the Mosaic Law, the Israelites were instructed to contribute a portion of their income, typically one-tenth, as tithes. These tithes were to be brought to a central place of worship, where the community would come together in a communal spirit to partake in communal meals, offer thanks to God for His provision, and engage in collective worship and celebration. This practice reinforced the spiritual connection among the Israelites and served as a tangible expression of their gratitude and devotion to their faith.

"There bring your burnt offerings and sacrifices, your tithes, and special gifts, what you have vowed to give and your freewill offerings, and the firstborn of your herds and flocks. There, in the presence of the Lord your God, you and your families shall eat and shall rejoice in everything you have put your hand to, because the Lord your God has blessed you."
Deuteronomy 12:6-7.

The book of Deuteronomy provides a detailed explanation of the communal aspect of tithing in the Bible. According to the text, the Israelites were instructed to bring their tithes and other offerings to the place God chose for his dwelling, the Tabernacle or the Temple. This act of bringing tithes and offerings was accompanied by communal meals and rejoicing, where the Israelites collectively acknowledged God's blessings and celebrated their shared faith in the presence of their father, the God Almighty.

The communal worship and tithing practice served several crucial functions in the community of believers. Firstly, it reinforced the nation's unity under God, as all the tribes would assemble in a central location to worship. This gathering allowed the Israelites to publicly acknowledge God's provision and share in the joy of His blessings with one another. The communal meals symbolized fellowship with one another and God, highlighting God as the ultimate provider. The Mosaic Law emphasized that giving was both a private transaction and a public expression of faith and thanksgiving. Furthermore, it connected the Israelites' material resources with their spiritual life, reminding them to dedicate all they had to the glory of God, as everything they possessed came from Him.

Bringing tithes to a central place of worship, such as the Tabernacle or Temple, was a sacred commandment in the Bible for the Israelites. It served as a way for the community to come together in the presence of God, offering thanksgiving and rejoicing in His blessings. This tradition continues to be celebrated today as people gather to fellowship and renew their commitment to their forefathers' covenant with God.

This act of communal worship, marked by the bringing of gifts to the house of God, has been explained by theologians as the practice of tithing. It was seen as a way to reinforce the unity of the nation under God and to remind the Israelites that their identity as a people is set apart for God's purposes. Participating in this communal worship reminds the people that their dependence lies on God alone, and they are called to honor Him with their lives and resources.

The Role of Tithing in the Spiritual and Social Life

Tithing played an important part in Israelite culture, funding the priesthood, assisting those in need, and creating communal bonds. These acts of generosity were more than just money support; they were closely connected with Israel's spiritual life, influencing many elements of Jewish life. Tithing was more than just an obligation; it was an act of devotion and obedience, recognizing that everything the Israelites owned belonged to God. This gesture indicated their faith, trust, and reverence for God, and by offering, they discovered a closer relationship with their Creator.

Moreover, tithing played a pivotal role in upholding the sanctity of the priesthood and the nation's worship practices. It was not just an act of obedience, worship, and reverence to God, but it also had practical implications. Tithing provided crucial support to the Levites, ensuring the continuity of religious rituals, sacrifices, and teachings. The Levites, as intermediaries between the children of Israel and God, relied on these offerings. The Israelites were instructed to set aside a portion of their produce and livestock, not just as a gesture of acknowledgment of God's sovereignty and provision, but as a practical means to sustain the religious structure of their society.

Spiritual, Social Role of Tithing

Tithing had a deep spiritual meaning for the Israelites. It was not only a reminder of God's supply and their full reliance on Him, but it was also a display of worship and obedience. By donating a share of their produce and cattle, the Israelites openly acknowledged that everything they owned was ultimately a God-given blessing. This act of giving was more than just a ritual; it was a sort of worship. It was a visible demonstration of their love and faith in God, strengthening their spiritual bond with their Creator. Their adherence to God's commands through tithing was an effective approach to strengthen their covenant bond with Him.

"Honor the Lord with your wealth, with the first fruits of all your crops; then your barns will be filled to overflowing, and your vats will brim over with new wine." Proverbs 3:9-10

The Proverbs echoes the sentiment that when people honor God with their resources will also bring blessings to them. Giving your substance to God is a principle that invite God's favor and provision to the believers. Tithing ensured that the less privileges of the community were met, particularly those of the Levites and the marginalized. The redistribution of resources through tithing created a system of care that reflected God's justice and compassion, and fostered a sense of community and responsibility, reminding the Israelites that their well-being was interconnected with that of their neighbors.

> *"Will a mere mortal rob God? Yet you rob me. But you ask, 'How are we robbing you?' In tithes and offerings. You are under a curse—your whole nation—because you are robbing me.*
> *Bring the whole tithe into the storehouse, that there may be food in my house. Test me in this," says the Lord Almighty, "and see if I will not throw open the floodgates of heaven and pour out so much blessing that there will not be room enough to store it. I will prevent pests from devouring your crops, and the vines in your fields will not drop their fruit before it is ripe," says the Lord Almighty. "Then all the nations will call you blessed, for yours will be a delightful land," says the Lord Almighty.*
> *"Will a mere mortal rob God? Yet you rob me. But you ask, 'How are we robbing you?' In tithes and offerings." Malachi 3:8-12 (NIV)*

The concept of tithing in the book of Malachi is a powerful illustration of the importance of faithfulness and obedience. In this passage, the prophet Malachi addresses the issue of people neglecting to bring their tithes and offerings to the storehouse. God confronts the Israelites with the accusation that they are robbing Him by withholding what rightfully belongs to Him. This serves as a reminder of the significance of honoring God with our finances and resources.

The term "robbing" underscores the idea that the Israelites were holding back something that was meant to be dedicated to God. According to the Mosaic Law, the tithe, representing a tenth of one's income or produce, was considered holy and set apart for the Lord. By failing to honor this practice, the Israelites neglected a fundamental religious duty and violated their covenant relationship with God. As a result, the entire nation of Israel was under a curse due to their disobedience in withholding tithes and offerings.

It explains the importance of honoring God with our resources and the consequences of neglecting this aspect of our relationship with Him. It encourages us to consider our faithfulness and obedience in praising God with our finances and resources. Neglecting to bring the whole tithe could lead to various challenges, such as poor harvests, economic difficulties, or other misfortunes. Failure to bring the entire tithe was not just a personal issue for the Israelites but a national problem with collective consequences. It reflects that disobedience to God's commands leads to adverse outcomes, while obedience brings blessings.

God's command to "bring the whole tithe into the storehouse" refers to supporting the community's Levites, priests, and poor. By challenging the Israelites to "test" Him in bringing the whole tithe, God offers a remarkable promise: if they are faithful in their tithing, God will pour out blessings so abundant that there will not be enough room to store them.

The metaphor of the "floodgates of heaven" symbolizes the promise of abundant rainfall, signifying plentiful harvests and economic prosperity. This divine promise reassures the Israelites that their commitment to tithing will result in blessings from God, reversing the curse and ushering in a season of abundance.

In addition to abundant blessings, God pledges protection, preventing pests from ravaging the crops and ensuring the vines bear fruit without premature loss. While some may interpret this message as directed solely at farmers, it's important to remember that agriculture was the primary livelihood for the Israelites at that time.

The significance of faithful tithing and the implications of neglecting this practice are underscored. God accuses the Israelites of robbing Him by withholding their tithes and offerings, which has brought a curse upon the nation. However, God also invites the people to test His faithfulness by bringing the entire tithe to the storehouse. If they honor this, He promises abundant blessings, protection for their crops, and the transformation of their land into a source of joy and prosperity that other nations will recognize.

This excerpt underscores the sacred agreement between God and His people, illustrating that obeying His commands results in blessings, while disobedience leads to hardships. It also emphasizes the interconnection between spiritual devotion and material prosperity, a principle that has reverberated throughout Israel's history and remains pertinent for contemporary believers. Safeguarding crops and guaranteeing a bountiful harvest symbolize God's direct intervention in the natural order to bestow blessings upon His people. Thus, it conveys that God has authority over nature and can choose to confer or withhold prosperity based on the faithfulness of His people.

Furthermore, the passage demonstrates that Israel's obedience extends beyond their immediate circumstances. It asserts that if the Israelites heed God's call and faithfully tithe, the resulting blessings will be so unmistakable that "all the nations" will acknowledge and commend Israel's prosperity. The phrase "Yours will be a delightful land" signifies the transformation that will occur when the Israelites return to God through faithful tithing. The land, once cursed, will be transformed into a place of abundance and joy, capturing the attention and admiration of other nations. This outcome reflects God's desire for Israel to serve as a testament to His benevolence and constancy, showcasing the rewards that stem from living in obedience to His decrees.

The Declaration of the Tithe: An Act of Faith

"When you have finished setting aside a tenth of all your produce in the third year, the year of the tithe, you shall give it to the Levite, the foreigner, the fatherless and the widow, so that they may eat in your towns and be satisfied. Then say to the Lord your God: 'I have removed from my house the sacred portion and have given it to the Levite, the foreigner, the fatherless and the widow, according to all you commanded. I have not turned aside from your commands nor have I forgotten any of them. I have not eaten any of the sacred portion while I was in mourning, nor have I removed any of it while I was unclean, nor have I offered any of it to the dead. I have obeyed the Lord my God; I have done everything you commanded me. Look down from heaven, your holy dwelling place, and bless your people Israel and the land you have given us as you promised on oath to our ancestors, a land flowing with milk and honey."
Deuteronomy 26:12-15

Moses decreed that the third year should be designated the "year of the tithe." According to this decree, the Israelites were instructed to allocate their tithes to the Levites, who had no land inheritance, as well as the foreigners, orphans, and widows. This allocation was to be accompanied by a solemn declaration before the Lord, affirming their commitment to obeying God's commands. This declaration expressed the Israelites' obedience and devotion to God, publicly acknowledging their adherence to God's instructions by setting aside a sacred portion for its intended purposes. By obeying this commandment, the Israelites sought God's continual blessings on the land and the people, recognizing that their prosperity depended entirely on God's favor.

Compliance with these directives underscores the spiritual significance of tithing as a sacred act to be observed in the consciousness of God's presence. This mindful approach, combined with strict adherence to His commands, ensures complete obedience and reflects the reverence with which the Israelites approached their relationship with God. It's important to note that these acts of giving demonstrate spiritual discipline and a tangible expression   of   faith.

Chapter 3

Jesus and Tithing: A New Perspective?

"Woe to you, teachers of the law and Pharisees, you hypocrites! You give a tenth of your spices—mint, dill, and cumin. But you have neglected the more important matters of the law—justice, mercy, and faithfulness. You should have practiced the latter, without neglecting the former." Matthew 23:23 (NIV)

The concept of tithing was addressed during Jesus' ministry as he critiqued the religious practices of his time, especially those of the Pharisees. Although the Pharisees were meticulous in their observance of the Law, including tithing, Jesus challenged them to consider the more profound principles underlying their religious duties. The book of Matthew delves into Jesus' teachings on tithing, focusing on his interactions with the Pharisees and how he instructed them on the true essence of tithing. Jesus rebuked the Pharisees for their hypocrisy in tithing. Known for their meticulous adherence to the Law, the Pharisees even tithed the most insignificant herbs from their gardens, such as mint, dill, and cumin, to demonstrate their commitment to fulfilling the letter of the Law. However, Jesus highlighted that while they were diligent in these minor matters, they neglected the "more important matters of the law"—justice, mercy, and faithfulness.

The Pharisees were known for their meticulous tithing and emphasis on external religious practices. They believed that by strictly following every detail of the Mosaic Law, including tithing, they could guarantee their righteousness in the eyes of God. However, this strict focus on legalistic righteousness led them to burden themselves and others, often overshadowing deeper spiritual values. Interestingly, the Pharisees went beyond what the Law of Moses required by tithing minor items like spices while tithing the mandated produce, grain, wine, oil, and livestock. However, this zealous devotion to the Law caused them to neglect the weightier matters at the core of God's commandments.

When Jesus addressed the Pharisees, he aimed to differentiate between their outward observance of religious practices and their internal commitment to the principles these practices were supposed to embody. While tithing was an essential part of the Law, it was not meant to be an end. Instead, it was intended to reflect a heart aligned with God's values—justice, mercy, and faithfulness. The teachings underline that tithing is about giving financially and embodying Christ-like qualities of justice, mercy, and faithfulness.

Justice encompasses fair and righteous treatment of others, particularly the poor, the marginalized, and the oppressed. In the teachings of prophets like Amos and Micah, there was a consistent call for Israel to practice justice as a fundamental requirement of their covenant with God. However, the people prioritized legalistic adherence to the Law over ensuring justice was served, especially for the vulnerable.

These teachings served as reminders of God's merciful nature. Jesus confronted religious leaders who were quick to judge but lacked compassion, emphasizing the importance of showing mercy and care for sinners and the poor. He also stressed the significance of loyalty and steadfastness in one's relationship with God and others, emphasizing the importance of being true to the spirit of the Law, not just its literal interpretation. The Pharisees Law focus on external observance caused them to overlook the essence of faithfulness – a wholehearted devotion to God and the embodiment of His commandments in all aspects of life. Giving tithes becomes a more joyful act by focusing on God's faithfulness.

In Matthew 23:23, Jesus emphasized the importance of tithing as part of the Law and highlighted the need to integrate tithing with broader aspects such as justice, mercy, and Faithfulness. While Jesus indicated that tithing is not the sole measure of righteousness, He underscored its significance within a comprehensive framework of obedience to God's commandments. He emphasized the necessity of genuine love for God and neighbor, challenging the mindset that prioritizes ritual observance over authentic spiritual values. Jesus called for a higher standard of living that encompasses God's values and transcends mere external compliance. This holistic approach encourages believers to integrate tithing with a sincere heart and motives as part of their obedience and spiritual values.

In Jesus's teachings, tithing is not dismissed as unnecessary. Rather, it is presented as a means of honoring God and fulfilling His purposes. However, Jesus emphasizes the importance of prioritizing justice, mercy, and faithfulness in conjunction with tithing. He prompts believers to assess their motives for tithing, encouraging sincere devotion to God rather than obligation or a desire for recognition. Jesus urges his followers to align their giving with a profound understanding of God's will and character.

Chapter 4

Tithing as a Call to Holistic Obedience

"Woe to you Pharisees, because you give God a tenth of your mint, rue and all other kinds of garden herbs, but you neglect justice and the love of God. You should have practiced the latter without leaving the former undone." Luke 11:42 (NIV)

Jesus calls on believers to move beyond mere ritualistic observance and instead embrace a comprehensive obedience encompassing justice, mercy, and faithfulness. Within this framework, tithing is part of a broader commitment to live out God's commandments in every aspect of our lives. Believers must remember that giving is not just a financial transaction, but a personal act of love for God. It should be rooted in a deep love for God and a sincere desire to reflect His justice, mercy, and faithfulness in the world. In this way, tithing becomes not merely a duty but a significant expression of our personal relationship with God and our dedication to His kingdom, fostering a deep spiritual connection.

In His teachings, Jesus often discusses the religious practices of the Pharisees and utilizes these discussions to impart deeper spiritual truths, including the practice of tithing. While the Pharisees were meticulous in their observance of tithing, Jesus teaches that tithing must be understood within the broader context of God's expectations for justice, mercy, and love, as conveyed in His interactions with the Pharisees, notably in Luke 11:42. Despite their diligence in tithing, the Pharisees are criticized for neglecting the weightier matters of the Law, such as justice and the love of God.

This underscores the moral weight of our actions in tithing, reminding us of the importance of justice, mercy, and love in our relationship with God.

The Pharisees were renowned for their strict adherence to the Law of Moses. They meticulously observed every detail of Law, including tithing, believing that they could attain righteousness before God by doing so. They even went as far as tithing the most minor elements of their produce. This practice exceeded the literal requirements of the Law, which focused primarily on tithing agricultural produce such as grain, wine, oil, and livestock. This emphasis on meticulous tithing reflects the Pharisees' broader approach to religion, prioritizing external actions and legalistic precision as indicators of their righteousness. However, in doing so, they often lost sight of the weightier matters that the law was intended to uphold — matters that speak to the heart of God's character and His expectations for His people.

Justice and the Love of God: The Weightier Matters

In Luke 11:42, Jesus criticizes the Pharisees, drawing attention to two fundamental principles they disregarded: justice and the love of God. This critique underscores the importance of practicing fairness and demonstrating genuine love for God in one's actions and attitudes.

Justice: In the Bible, justice is not just a concept, but a profound principle that is often associated with fairness, righteousness, and the equitable treatment of others, especially the poor, the marginalized, and the oppressed. The prophets of the Old Testament, such as Isaiah, Amos, and Micah, repeatedly called Israel to practice justice, emphasizing that faithful obedience to God involved caring for those who were vulnerable and ensuring that everyone was treated fairly. In their focus on the minutiae of the Law, the Pharisees were failing to live out this crucial aspect of God's commandments.

The Love of God: The love of God is not a mere sentiment, but a profound reality that encompasses a deep, personal devotion to God and a commitment to reflect His love in how one treats others. This principle is central to Jesus' teachings, where He summarizes the Law and the Prophets with the commandments to love God with all one's heart, soul, and mind and to love one's neighbor as oneself (Matthew 22:37-40). The Pharisees, however, were so focused on outward religious practices that they neglected this foundational principle of love, both in their relationship with God and in their interactions with others.

The Pharisees, by neglecting justice and the love of God, were missing the true purpose of the Law. Jesus did not dismiss the practice of tithing; he mentioned that they 'should have practiced the latter without leaving the former undone.' However, He emphasized that tithing becomes an empty ritual without being connected to the more significant principles of justice and love. Tithing, when done with a heart for justice, is a tangible expression of our love for God and our concern for the well-being of others.

The question of whether Jesus upheld, or redefined tithing is nuanced. In Luke 11:42, Jesus does not explicitly abolish tithing; he acknowledges its place in religious practice. Nevertheless, his emphasis on justice and the love of God suggests that tithing must be understood within a broader context of ethical and spiritual responsibility.

Tithing as Part of a Greater Whole

Jesus' teachings suggest that while tithing is a critical practice, it should not be viewed as the sole measure of righteousness. Instead, it is an essential part of a life fully dedicated to following God's commandments, primarily how we treat others and show our love for God. Jesus' critique of the Pharisees does not mean a rejection of tithing but rather a call for a more comprehensive approach to obeying God's will. Tithing should reflect a heart in harmony with God's values, particularly His concern for justice and His call to love.

The teaching of Jesus stresses that tithing should originate from a genuine desire to uphold justice, show mercy, and demonstrate love for God. When approached with sincerity, tithing becomes a significant manifestation of faith.

This perspective compels believers to scrutinize their motives for tithing. Are they giving out of a sense of duty, habit, or the need to appear righteous? Or are they expressing their love for God and dedication to His principles of justice and mercy? Jesus calls on His followers to ensure that their tithing, along with all other religious practices, springs from an authentic aspiration to embody God's character and honor His commandments. In Luke 11:42, the challenge is to move beyond the mere mechanics of religious observance and embrace a deeper, more comprehensive approach to faith.

Although Jesus did not abolish tithing, He emphasized that it should be practiced harmoniously with the weightier matters of justice and the love of God. For present-day believers, this means that tithing should not be perceived as an end but as part of a broader commitment to God's commandments in all aspects of life. When we tithe, we should do so with a heart devoted to justice, mercy, and love – values that lie at the core of God's character and the teachings of Jesus. These transforms tithing from a mere religious duty into a profound expression of our faith and allegiance to God's kingdom, inspiring us to live out these values in all aspects of our lives.

Jesus often spoke about wealth, giving, and one's heart toward God. Tithing was a subject of direct and indirect discussion, especially in Jesus' interactions with the Pharisees and His teachings on giving. Illustration on the widow's offering in MaJesus'41-44 and his discourse on laying up treasures in heaven in Matthew 6:19-21 reflect more profound principles of justice, mercy, and faithfulness.

"Jesus sat down opposite the place where the offerings were put and watched the crowd putting their money into the temple treasury. Many rich people threw in large amounts. But a poor widow came and put in two very small copper coins, worth only a few cents. Calling his disciples to him, Jesus said, 'Truly I tell you; this poor widow has put more into the treasury than all the others. They all gave out of their wealth; but she, out of her poverty, put in everything—all she had to live on." Mark 12:41-44 (NIV)

A Contrast in Giving: The Rich vs. The Widow
Jesus was witnessing people making donations to the temple
treasury. Many affluent individuals contributed significant quantities
of money. However, Jesus spotted a poor widow who deposited two
little copper pennies worth very little. Despite the low value of her
donation, Jesus praised her, saying she had contributed more than
all the others since she gave from her poverty, offering everything
she had to survive on. The widow's donation contrasted sharply with
the wealthy's giving. While the wealthy donated generously, their
giving was commensurate to their abundance. For them, the
contributions, while significant, were not sacrificial; they were giving
from their surplus. In contrast, the widow's offering was a true
sacrifice. She gave all that she had, holding nothing back for herself.
Her act of sacrifice is a testament to her deep faith and devotion.

This compelling contrast underscores a fundamental principle in
Jesus' teachings: the worth of an offering is not gauged by its
quantity but by the sincerity and selflessness behind it. Despite being
modest, the widow's gift symbolizes complete surrender and
unwavering trust in God. Her act of giving all she has is a powerful
demonstration of faith in God's ability to meet her needs. The
widow's giving is in harmony with the biblical principle that
authentic giving requires sacrifice and emanates from a heart filled
with faith and dedication. According to Jesus, giving—whether in
tithes, offerings, or alms—holds significance only when it mirrors a
genuine devotion to God. This teaching redefines giving,
transcending mere compliance with a legal obligation (such as
tithing), and delving into the giver's innermost intentions. Jesus does
not downplay the importance of giving but underscores that the
spirit in which one gives surpasses the significance of the amount

given. The widow's offering epitomizes the giving that delights God—a giving that is wholehearted, sacrificial, and rooted in unwavering trust.

Treasure in Heaven: A Call to Prioritize Eternal Values

"Do not store up for yourselves treasures on earth, where moths and vermin destroy, and where thieves break in and steal. But store up for yourselves treasures in heaven, where moths and vermin do not destroy, and where thieves do not break in and steal. For where your treasure is, there your heart will be also." Matthew 6:19-21 (NIV)

In his Sermon on the Mount, Jesus teaches the correct attitude toward wealth and material possessions. He warns against hoarding "treasures on earth," which are fleeting and vulnerable to corrosion and theft. Instead, Jesus instructs His disciples to "store up treasures in heaven," where they would be safe and endure. The following phrase captures the essence of this teaching: "For where your treasure is, there your heart will be also." Tithing, when regarded in this manner, is more than merely completing a religious duty; it is also about aligning one's heart with God's kingdom. By giving to God and investing in His work, believers are "storing up treasures in heaven." This concept suggests that tithing should be considered as part of a broader commitment to use one's resources for purposes that hold eternal significance.

Jesus' instruction on accumulating treasures in heaven encourages believers to examine their values and priorities. Whether through tithing, offerings, or charitable deeds, giving reveals one's most cherished values. If one's treasure is in earthly wealth, one's heart will be attached to temporary and ultimately insecure things. However, if their treasure is in heaven, their hearts will focus on God and eternal things. This teaching challenges believers to see tithing as a financial transaction and a spiritual discipline reflecting their ultimate allegiance. In this sense, Jesus is not just endorsing the practice of tithing but is redefining it within the broader context of discipleship and the pursuit of God's kingdom.

A Heart-Centered Approach to Giving

Jesus underscores that the value of giving does not lie solely in the amount given or fulfilling a duty but in the orientation of the heart towards God. He calls His followers to give sacrificially, akin to the widow, and invest in eternal treasures rather than earthly ones. This heart-centered approach shifts the focus from legalistic adherence to the Law to a deeper spiritual practice that reflects a more profound love for God and dedication to His kingdom. According to Jesus, tithing is just one part of a broader spiritual discipline that encompasses justice, mercy, faithfulness, and love. It's not just about giving a tenth of one's income but prioritizing God's values over worldly ones. This redefinition compels believers to scrutinize their motives, give with a heart entirely devoted to God, and perceive their giving as a reflection of their trust in His provision and their commitment to His eternal purposes.

Jesus' teachings on giving, as seen in the stories of the widow's offering and the encouragement to store up treasures in heaven, offer a fresh perspective on tithing. While Jesus doesn't explicitly abolish the practice of tithing, He reframes it within the context of wholehearted devotion, sacrificial giving, and the pursuit of eternal values. This indicates that tithing should not be seen purely as a religious duty but as an opportunity to express trust in God, love for Him, and dedication to His kingdom. The accurate measure of giving is not in quantity but in its heartfelt intention— an intention that aims to honor God, benefit others, and invest in lasting principles. This way, tithing transforms from a mere obligation into a profound demonstration of faith and an essential component of a life devoted to God's purposes.

Chapter 5

Tithing in the Early Church: Practice and Evolution

"All the believers were together and had everything in common. They sold property and possessions to give to anyone who had need." Acts 2:44-45 (NIV)

The early Christian community, which arose in the years following Jesus' resurrection and ascension, had the huge difficulty of reconciling Old Testament rituals, such as tithe, with the new covenant created by Christ. As the Church grew and adapted to many cultures and areas, giving and community support principles evolved significantly.

This chapter delves into the early Christian approach to tithing and giving, focusing on key examples from the Acts of the Apostles and the Pauline epistles. Furthermore, the chapter will investigate how the practice of tithe was contextualized and evolved within the New Testament church. One remarkable aspect of the early Christian community, documented in the Book of Acts, is their profound commitment to sharing resources and providing support to one another. This commitment extended beyond traditional tithing practices, reflecting a deep-rooted sense of unity and mutual responsibility within the community.

Commonality and Generosity

"All the believers were together and had everything in common. [45] They sold property and possessions to give to anyone who had need". Acts 2:44-45

In the early days of the Church, remarkable unity and solidarity were evident among believers. They lived in close-knit communities, sharing not only their lives but also their material possessions. This radical display of generosity was manifested in the communal sharing of resources, with individuals willingly selling their property and possessions to support those in need. Notably, there was no set percentage for giving; instead, the early Christians were responsive to the needs of their community and sought guidance from the Holy Spirit. Their act of giving was a profound demonstration of their commitment to fulfilling religious obligations, an outward expression of their deep love for one another, and their earnest desire to embody the teachings of Jesus.

"A new command I give you: Love one another. As I have loved you, so you must love one another. [35] By this everyone will know that you are my disciples if you love one another." John 13:34-35.

The early Church's approach to giving was deeply rooted in the teachings of Jesus. Jesus had commanded his followers to love one another as He had loved them (John 13:34-35). This love was intended to be expressed through concrete actions, including meeting the material needs of fellow believers. The early Christians were unified in their commitment to this command, seeing themselves as part of one body. This shared identity and purpose motivated them to prioritize the community's needs over individual wealth and possessions. As a result, the early Christian community embraced a culture of generosity and selflessness, reflecting the love and compassion modeled by Jesus.

The Evolution of Giving in the Early Church

"Remember this: Whoever sows sparingly will also reap sparingly, and whoever sows generously will also reap generously. Each of you should give what you have decided in your heart to give, not reluctantly or under compulsion, for God loves a cheerful giver." 2 Corinthians 9:6-7 (NIV)

The early Church expanded beyond Jerusalem, and the practice of giving continued to develop. The Apostle Paul played a crucial role in shaping the early Christian understanding of giving, transitioning it from tithing to a broader concept of generosity and support for the Church and its mission. In his epistles, Paul provides several essential teachings on giving, emphasizing generosity, willingness, and giving according to one's ability. These principles reflect a move away from strict adherence to tithing as a fixed percentage and towards a more flexible and grace-filled approach to giving. For Paul, giving is a response to God's grace and is motivated by love and a desire to support the work of the gospel.

Generosity: Paul encourages believers to give generously, understanding that their giving will result in blessings for themselves and others. The metaphor of sowing and reaping suggests that the measure of one's giving will directly influence the blessings one receives.

Willingness: Paul emphasizes that giving should be done willingly, not out of reluctance or compulsion. This reflects a shift from the legalistic requirement of tithing to a more voluntary and heartfelt practice.

Cheerfulness: The attitude of the giver is crucial. Paul stresses that God loves a cheerful giver, implying that the spirit in which one gives is as important as the act of giving itself.

Supporting the Church and Its Mission

The early Church had a tradition of providing financial support to missionaries, church leaders, and fellow believers. This support was especially crucial for those who were facing hardship. Apostle Paul, a key figure in the early Christian Church, was known for organizing collections to assist low-income individuals. His efforts focused on helping the believers in Jerusalem experiencing famine and persecution. Paul encouraged the Corinthian believers to make regular financial contributions to support the needs of the Church. This demonstrated an organized and intentional approach to giving, emphasizing the importance of planning and consistency in contributing to the community. Paul's guidance highlighted that believers should give according to their means, promoting a fair and sustainable support system within the Church.

"Now about the collection for the Lord's people: Do what I told the Galatian churches to do. On the first day of every week, each one of you should set aside a sum of money in keeping with your income, saving it up, so that when I come no collections will have to be made." 1 Corinthians 16:1-2 (NIV)

The early Church had a communal approach to giving, with collections serving local congregations and the entire Christian community. This interconnectedness of the churches demonstrated the early Christians' collective responsibility to care for one another, regardless of their geographic or cultural differences. While the importance of giving remained central, the strict requirement of tithing as prescribed in the Old Testament was not directly carried over into the New Testament Church. Instead, giving was tailored to accommodate the new covenant realities and the unique needs of the Christian community.

Furthermore, early Christians recognized that their giving was not simply about meeting a legal requirement but rather about actively participating in the work of God's kingdom. This shift in perspective allowed for a more flexible and generous approach to giving, one motivated by love, unity, and a desire to support the Church's mission. In contrast to the fixed percentage of the Old Testament tithe, the New Testament encouraged believers to give according to their ability and willingness, placing importance on the intent behind the gift. This shift in practice reflects the broader New Testament theme of grace prevailing over the law, emphasizing the spirit of the law rather than its letter.

The early Church's approach to giving was deeply rooted in the role of the Holy Spirit. Guided by the Holy Spirit, early Christians displayed spontaneous and responsive generosity towards others. This Spirit-led giving often led to radical acts, such as selling possessions to support the community, as in Acts 2:44-45. Relying on the Holy Spirit made giving more personalized and attuned to the unique circumstances of each believer and community. Instead of a one-size-fits-all approach, giving in the early Church was dynamic and adaptable, allowing for diverse expressions of God's love and provision.

The early Christian community's approach to giving marked a significant departure from the Old Testament practice of tithing. While the essential principles of supporting God's work and caring for those in need remained central, the early Church embraced a more generous, voluntary, and Spirit-led model of giving. This approach was characterized by radical generosity, a strong sense of community, and a focus on the Church's broader mission. As giving evolved within the New Testament Church, it became less about meeting a specific quota and more about embodying the love, unity, and generosity advocated by Jesus. The example set by the early Church challenges contemporary believers to view giving not merely as a duty but as an opportunity to participate in God's work, support one another, and reflect the grace received through Christ.

The Book of Acts exemplified a distinctive approach to communal living and giving that mirrored the gospel's transformative power in their lives. The early Christian community's radical approach to ownership and generosity highlighted several critical aspects of their communal lifestyle, directly influenced by their faith in Jesus Christ and commitment to living out His teachings. The early Church practiced tithing and giving, primarily focusing on the communal lifestyle described in Acts 4:32-35. This passage provides profound insight into the early Church's generosity and how their approach to sharing resources went beyond traditional tithing to embody the principles of unity, love, and mutual support.

"All the believers were one in heart and mind. No one claimed that any of their possessions was their own, but they shared everything they had. With great power the apostles continued to testify to the resurrection of the Lord Jesus. And God's grace was so powerfully at work in them all that there were no needy persons among them. For from time to time those who owned land or houses sold them, brought the

money from the sales and put it at the apostles' feet, and it was distributed to anyone who had need." Acts 4:32-35 (NIV)

The book of Acts emphasizes the unity of the believers, stating that "All the believers were united in heart and mind." This unity went beyond mere agreement and was a deep spiritual connection rooted in their shared faith in Jesus. Their common belief in Christ's resurrection and commitment to His teachings created a bond that transcended social, economic, and cultural differences. This unity of heart and mind formed the foundation of their communal lifestyle, fostering an environment where believers freely shared their resources, and the community's needs took precedence over individual desires. The early Christians recognized that they belonged to a new spiritual family, the body of Christ, and this understanding drove their commitment to one another.

A notable feature of the early Church, as described in Acts 4:32-35, is their approach to possessions. "No one claimed that any of their possessions was their own, but they shared everything they had." This statement reflects a substantial shift in how the early Christians viewed their material wealth. Instead of considering their possessions as personal property to be hoarded, they regarded them as communal resources to be used for the entire community's benefit.

This spirit of radical generosity naturally stemmed from their unity and deep commitment to living as disciples. They viewed their possessions as divine gifts meant to be used to support the needs of the community. This mindset led to a selfless attitude towards their wealth, where they were willing to sell their property and belongings to ensure that everyone in the community was cared for.

"Occasionally, those who owned land or houses would sell them, donate the proceeds, and entrust the funds to the apostles, who would then distribute them to those in need." This practice of selling property for the greater good was driven by love and empathy rather than being a compulsory act of giving. It spontaneously demonstrated the believers' dedication to supporting each other.

The Role of the Apostles

The apostles played a vital role in the communal lifestyle by overseeing the fair distribution of resources. When believers sold their property, they brought the proceeds to the apostles, who distributed the funds to those in need. This ensured that resources were allocated according to the community's needs. The members trusted the apostles to manage the communal resources wisely and justly, using the wealth to support the vulnerable and meet the needs of the entire community. Encouraging these acts in the church community can help build the trust exhibited in the early Church.

Another lesson to be learned is the acknowledgment that "God's grace was so powerfully at work in them all that there were no needy persons among them." The early Church's radical form of generosity and communal living directly resulted from God's grace at work in their lives. This grace empowered the believers to transcend cultural norms of ownership and wealth, prioritizing the needs of others over personal gain. The grace-filled community became a powerful witness to the transformative impact of the gospel, embodying the love and unity that Jesus had taught.

The communal lifestyle of the early Church, as depicted in Acts 4:32-35, presents a profound understanding of Christian generosity and the significance of community living. This passage illustrates the unity and sharing among the believers, emphasizing their collective support and care for one another.

The early Christians' approach to possessions and wealth mirrored the values of the Kingdom of God. In the Kingdom, material wealth was not seen as the ultimate goal but rather as a resource to be used for the benefit of others. The early Church exemplified this value by sharing its resources and ensuring that no one was left in need.

The passage emphasizes the concept of stewardship. Believers acknowledged that their possessions ultimately belonged to God and were entrusted to them for the purpose of serving others. This understanding of stewardship formed the basis of their willingness to share and give sacrificially.

The unity, generosity, and mutual care the early Christian community displayed served as a compelling testimony to the surrounding world. Their communal lifestyle was a tangible expression of the gospel, demonstrating that the love of Christ could overcome barriers and establish a new kind of community where everyone was esteemed and looked after.

The Evolution of Giving in the Early Church

The early Church expanded beyond Jerusalem and became more diverse. While the principles of communal living and radical generosity continued to influence Christian practice, they adapted to the needs of different communities. Although communal living, as described in Acts 4:32-35, was unique to the Jerusalem church, the core values of generosity, unity, and caring for the needy remained integral to the life of the Church. The letters of the Apostle Paul to the churches reflect the ongoing significance of generosity and communal support and the adaptation of these practices to different contexts. Paul urged the believers in the Gentile churches to give generously, not because they had to, but because they were willing and in response to God's grace.

In 2 Corinthians' 8:1-5, Paul commends the Macedonian churches for their generosity, even amid severe trial and poverty. He uses their example to encourage the Corinthian believers to give generously, emphasizing that their giving should be voluntary and motivated by love.

> *"Now about the collection" for the Lord's people: Do what the Galatian churches do. On the first day of every week, each of you should set aside a sum of money in keeping with your income, saving it up so that when I come, no collections will have to be made." 1 Corinthians 16:1-2*

The early Christian communities varied in their approaches to giving, with the Jerusalem church practicing communal living. In contrast, others, like the Corinthian Church, adopted a more systematic appeal. According to Paul's instructions in 1 Corinthians 16:1-2, the Corinthian believers were urged to contribute regularly and according to their means. This shift in giving practices allowed the early Church to adapt to different circumstances while upholding the values of generosity, unity, and care for the needy. Paul's guidance exemplifies a practical and organized approach to giving, balancing generosity with planning. As the early Church expanded and diversified, giving practices adapted to the needs of different congregations. Paul's instructions to the Corinthian Church regarding a collection for the believers in Jerusalem is an illustration of this. In 1 Corinthians 16:1-2.

The communal lifestyle of the early Church, as depicted in Acts 4:32-35, illustrates how the gospel can reshape a community's approach to wealth, possessions, and generosity. Although not all Christian communities may replicate this specific model of communal living, the underlying principles – unity, radical generosity, stewardship, and above all, care for the needy – remain fundamental to Christian practice. The early Church's approach to giving naturally flowed from their faith in Christ and their experience of God's grace. Their practices challenged the cultural norms of their time and served as a powerful testament to the gospel's transformative power. As the Church expanded and adapted to different contexts, these principles persisted in shaping the practice of giving, ensuring that the Church remained a community where all needs were met. The love of Christ was visibly demonstrated.

"Contemporary believers can find inspiration in the early Church's model, which challenges us to reconsider our attitudes towards possessions and charitable giving. It encourages us to explore ways to embody the same ethos of generosity, unity, and compassion within our communities, utilizing our resources not only for our benefit but also for the betterment of others and the glory of God. The collection referenced in 1 Corinthians 16:1-2 was part of a larger endeavor by Paul to gather financial assistance for the impoverished Christian community in Jerusalem. This effort was not exclusive to Corinth; Paul had issued directives similar to those of other congregations, including those in Galatia (as noted in the text), Macedonia, and Achaia (Romans 15:26)."

The collection was prompted by the economic challenges the believers in Jerusalem faced, possibly arising from factors such as famine, persecution, and the strain placed on local resources by their early communal living. Paul, deeply worried about the well-being of the Jerusalem church, viewed this collection as an opportunity for Gentile believers to demonstrate unity with their Jewish counterparts in Christ. This solidarity, this sense of being part of a larger community, would help fortify the Church's unity across cultural and geographical divides.

A Systematic Approach to Weekly Giving

Paul's instructions to the Corinthians include setting aside a sum of money weekly, specifically on the first day of the week. This regular practice was intended to be a fundamental part of their financial management. The instruction also emphasized the concept of giving in proportion to one's income, signifying that everyone's contribution should align with their financial capacity. This principle of proportional giving is significant for several reasons, as it encourages fair and equitable participation in supporting the community and its endeavors.

Regularity: Encouraging believers to give weekly, Paul introduced a structured and consistent approach to giving. This regularity ensured that the collection would steadily grow over time, making it possible to accumulate a substantial amount by the time Paul arrived to collect it. Regular giving also helped the believers develop a habit of generosity and kept the needs of the broader Christian community at the forefront of their minds.

Integration with Worship: Sunday, the "first day of the week," was when the early Christians gathered for worship to commemorate Jesus' resurrection. By linking the collection to their weekly worship, Paul integrated financial stewardship with their spiritual practice, reinforcing that giving was an act of prayer and a tangible expression of their faith.

Avoiding Last-Minute Collections: Paul's weekly instruction to set aside money was also practical. By saving up gradually, the Corinthians could avoid the pressure and potential embarrassment of scrambling to gather funds at the last minute when Paul arrived. This approach ensured the collection would be ready and organized, reflecting a thoughtful and responsible attitude towards giving.

Equity and Fairness: Basing contributions on income, Paul ensured that the burden of giving was distributed equitably among the congregation's members. Those with more significant financial resources could contribute more, while those with less could give according to their ability. This approach prevented financial strain on poorer members while still allowing everyone to participate in the collective effort.

Flexibility: Proportional giving allowed for flexibility in how individuals contributed, acknowledging that not everyone had the same financial capacity. This approach emphasized the importance of the heart and willingness to give rather than the specific amount. It also aligned with the broader New Testament principle that giving should be done cheerfully and not under compulsion (2 Corinthians 9:7).

Encouragement of Generosity: By not setting a fixed amount or percentage, Paul encouraged believers to consider their circumstances and to give generously according to their means. This method fostered a spirit of generosity and personal responsibility, allowing each believer to respond to the needs of the Church in a way that reflected their commitment and gratitude to God.

Paul's instructions in 1 Corinthians 16:1-2 highlight several crucial theological principles that contributed to the early Church's understanding of giving:

Stewardship and Responsibility: Paul's emphasis on regular, proportional giving reflects the early Christian belief in stewardship. Believers were called to manage their resources in a way that honored God and supported the community. This responsibility extended beyond their local congregation to include the broader body of Christ, demonstrating the interconnectedness of the early Church.

Unity and Solidarity: The collection for the Jerusalem church went beyond meeting financial needs; it served as a powerful expression of unity and solidarity among early Christians. By contributing to the needs of their distant brothers and sisters, the Gentile believers in Corinth were participating in the Church's broader mission and affirming their shared identity in Christ.

Worship and Generosity: Paul linked the collection to weekly worship, emphasizing that giving was integral to the Christian life. It was not merely a financial obligation, but an expression of prayer rooted in gratitude for God's grace and a desire to support His work. This perspective encouraged believers to view their giving as a joyful and meaningful service to God and others.

The Evolution of Giving in the Early Church

Paul's instructions in 1 Corinthians 16:1-2 mark a significant evolution in the early Church's approach to giving. While the Old Testament focused on tithing as a specific percentage, the New Testament Church, under Paul's guidance, transitioned towards a more flexible and generous approach to financial stewardship.

Let's explore the principles of generosity and systematic giving in the early Church. The shift from fixed tithing to proportional, voluntary giving allowed the Church to meet the diverse needs of its members. Paul's approach encouraged believers to give generously and sustainably, reflecting their commitment to God's work without imposing undue burdens on anyone.

Paul's guidance also emphasizes the role of the Church in managing and distributing resources. By organizing the collection and ensuring transparent handling, Paul demonstrated the importance of accountability and good stewardship within the Christian community. This approach helped build trust among believers and ensured the effective use of funds to support those in need.

The legacy of Paul's instructions for the collection in 1 Corinthians 16:1-2 provides valuable insights into the early Church's approach to giving. Paul's instructions reflect a thoughtful and organized approach to financial stewardship, emphasizing regular, proportional giving integrated with worship and motivated by a desire to support the broader Christian community. This passage also illustrates the transition in giving from the Old Testament practice of tithing to a New Testament model of generosity and flexibility. Paul's guidance continues to offer a powerful example for modern Christians, encouraging us to approach our giving with intentionality, generosity, and a deep sense of responsibility to God and His Church.

For contemporary believers, Paul's instructions challenge us to consider how to apply these principles in our lives. By setting aside resources regularly, giving according to our means, and viewing our financial stewardship as an act of worship, we can participate in the ongoing mission of the Church and reflect God's love and grace in tangible ways.

The Principle of Cheerful Giving

"Remember this: Whoever sows sparingly will also reap sparingly, and whoever sows generously will also reap generously. Each of you should give what you have decided in your heart to give, not reluctantly or under compulsion, for God loves a cheerful giver." 2 Corinthians 9:6-7 (NIV)

The early Christian Church continued to develop the principles of giving that reflect the teachings of Jesus Christ and the apostles. One of these teachings on giving is found in Paul's second letter to the Corinthians. In 2 Corinthians 9:6-7, Paul discusses the principle of cheerful giving and offers insights into the motivations and attitudes that should underlie Christian generosity. Paul also addresses the Corinthian church as part of his efforts to organize a collection for the impoverished believers in Jerusalem. The apostle delves into the mindset that believers should have when approaching generosity. Paul uses the agricultural principle of sowing and reaping as a metaphor familiar to the audience, explaining how the measure with which one sows will affect one's harvest.

"Whoever sows sparingly will also reap sparingly, and whoever sows generously will also reap generously." Here, sowing represents the act of giving, while reaping represents the blessings or returns from that giving. Paul emphasizes that generosity begets generosity, encouraging believers to give freely and abundantly to receive God's abundant blessings in return, not only in terms of finances but also spiritually and relationally.

Generosity as a Heart Condition

It's essential to remember Paul's analogy of sowing and reaping. It does not promote a transactional approach to giving, where one gives to receive material wealth. Instead, it emphasizes the need for the right mindset when giving. Generosity should flow from a heart aligned with God's principles and take joy in giving as an expression of love and faith. This concept resonates with the broader biblical teaching that God values the intentions and attitudes behind our actions. Therefore, the size of the gift is less important than the spirit in which it is given. A person giving a small amount with great joy and faith may be sowing more generously than someone giving a large amount grudgingly or out of obligation.

Voluntary and Thoughtful Giving

Paul encourages believers to give what they have "decided in your heart to give." Understanding the significance of this phrase and aligning it with the believers' values will help the church comprehend the essence of giving.

Voluntariness: Paul emphasizes that giving should be voluntary. It should not be about meeting a legal requirement or giving under pressure from others. Instead, it should stem from a personal, heartfelt decision to give based on one's relationship with God and understanding of His will.

Thoughtfulness: The instruction to decide in one's heart implies that giving should be thoughtful and intentional. It should not be a hasty or impulsive act but something that believers carefully consider, considering their resources, the needs of others, and how the Holy Spirit leads them.

Individual Responsibility: Paul's approach respects individual circumstances and freedom. He acknowledges that each person's ability to give will differ, and he does not impose a standard amount or percentage. Instead, he leaves it to each believer to decide, in consultation with God, what they are able and willing to contribute.

Avoiding Reluctance and Compulsion

Paul emphasizes that giving should not be done "reluctantly or under compulsion." Reluctant giving suggests a lack of wholeheartedness, where the giver may feel obligated or pressured but is not genuinely willing. Compulsory giving occurs when individuals think they have no choice or are coerced by others. Both attitudes are counterproductive to the giving that pleases God. When giving is reluctant or forced, it loses its value as an expression of love and faith. Instead of bringing joy to the giver and blessing the recipient, it can lead to resentment and a sense of loss. Paul's teaching underscores that true generosity comes from a place of freedom and joy, not from obligation or guilt.

The central idea of Paul's teaching in this passage culminates in the "statement, "For God loves a cheerful giver." This phrase captures the essence of Christian giving. T "The term "cheerful" derives from the Greek words "hi," various," and c," giving a sense of joyful, willing, and enthusiastic generosity. A cheerful giver takes pleasure in giving and views it as an opportunity rather than a burden. This teaching reflects the nature of God Himself, who epitomizes generous giving. God's love for God's wise giver is grounded in such generosity, mirroring His own. Just as God freely and joyfully gives to His children, He desires that His followers do the same, reflecting His character to the world. The principle of cheerful giving also emphasizes the relational aspect of giving. It is more than just a transaction between the giver and the recipient; it is an act of worship that strengthens the relationship between the giver and God. When believers give cheerfully, they engage in a divine economy in which the value of the gift is magnified by the love and joy with which it is given.

Paul's teachings of thoughtful giving in 2 Corinthians 9:6-7 carry significant theological implications for the practice of giving in the early Church and for believers today. Cheerful giving aligns with the New Testament's theme of grace. Just as God is free and cannot be earned, Christian giving should be a free and joyful response to that grace, shared willingly with others. This approach to providing contrasts with the Old Testament practice of tithing as a legal requirement and instead encourages believers to give as an expression of the grace they have received. Joy is seen as an indicator of spiritual health. The call to provide cheerfully suggests that finding joy in giving indicates spiritual health and maturity. When believers can give joyfully, it reflects a deep God's provision and a heart aligned with His purposes. Conversely, reluctance or compulsion in giving may indicate that one's relationship with God or understanding of His provision needs growth.

Model of Partnership

As the early Christian community grew and the gospel's message spread across the Roman Empire, providing financial support for the work of ministry became increasingly crucial. An exemplary illustration of this can be seen in the relationship between the apostle Paul and the church in Philippi, as documented in Philippians 4:15-18. This particular passage offers valuable insights into the early Christians' deep understanding of financial contributions' significance in supporting ministry. It portrays their recognition that giving was a practical necessity and a profound spiritual act of worship.

"Moreover, as you Philippians know, in the early days of your acquaintance with the gospel, when I set out from Macedonia, not one church shared with me in the matter of giving and receiving, except you only; for even when I was in Thessalonica, you sent me aid more than once when I was in need. Not that I desire your gifts; what I desire is that more be credited to your account. I have received full payment and have more than enough. I am amply supplied, now that I have received from Epaphroditus the gifts you sent. They are a fragrant offering, an acceptable sacrifice, pleasing to God."
Philippians 4:15-18 (NIV)

The profound connection between Paul and the Philippian Church explained the vital role of their financial support in sustaining the ministry. Paul's expressions convey his deep appreciation for their generosity and his recognition of the spiritual significance of their contributions. Paul begins by acknowledging the exceptional support he received from the Philippian Church. He points out that in the early stages of their introduction to the gospel when he departed from Macedonia, no other church participated "in the matter of giving and receiving" except the Philippians. This statement underscores Paul's unique bond with the Philippian believers, who willingly provided financial support even when other churches did not. The phrase "giving and receiving" implies a reciprocal relationship.

While the Philippians offered financial assistance, they also received spiritual blessings from Paul's ministry. This partnership was transactional and deeply relational, reflecting a mutual commitment to spreading the gospel. Paul further emphasizes the Philippians' kindness by recalling how they sent him to aid on multiple occasions, even during his time in Thessalonica. Their consistent support illustrates their enduring care for Paul's well-being and their steadfast dedication to advancing the mission of the Church.

Spiritual Significance of Giving

Paul is thankful for the gifts from the Philippians, yet he emphasizes that his main concern is not the material benefit he receives but the spiritual impact of their generosity. He states, "Not that I desire your gifts; what I desire is that more be credited to your account." This statement reflects Paul's view of giving as a spiritual investment. By using the language of accounting—"credited to your account"— Paul conveys the idea that the Philippians' generosity will result in spiritual rewards rather than material wealth. This aligns with the biblical teaching that God honors and rewards those who give generously out of love and faith.

Paul's emphasis on the spiritual benefits of giving also underscores the idea that giving is an act of worship. Through supporting Paul's ministry, the Philippians participated in the work of the gospel and aligned themselves with God's purposes. Their gifts were more than mere financial transactions; they were offerings that reflected their commitment to God and His mission.

Fragrant Offering and Acceptable Sacrifice

"The Lord smelled the pleasing aroma and said in his heart: "Never again will I curse the ground because of humans, even though every inclination of the human heart is evil from childhood. And never again will I destroy all living creatures, as I have done.

Paul further elevates the spiritual significance of the Philippians' gifts by describing them as "a fragrant offering, an acceptable sacrifice, pleasing to God." This imagery is rich with Old" (Genesis 8:21)

Paul emphasizes to the Philippians that their financial support is more than just a practical necessity; it is a sacred act. He parallels their giving and sacrifice on the altar, symbolizing their devotion to God and willingness to contribute to His work. This perspective raises giving to the level of worship, where the material support of ministry becomes a tangible expression of their faith and love for God.

The idea of a "fragrant offering" also suggests that their giving brings joy to God. Just as the aroma of a sacrifice was pleasing to the Lord in the Old Testament, so too is the generosity of believers when it is motivated by love and faith; this strengthens the belief that giving, when done with the right heart, is not merely a duty but a delightful offering to God.

Paul's Contentment and God's Provision

Paul is deeply grateful for the Philippians' support; he also expresses his contentment in God's provision. He states, "I have received full payment and have more than enough. I am amply supplied, now that I have received from Epaphroditus the gifts you sent." Paul's contentment is rooted in his trust in God's provision, rather than in the gifts themselves.

Earlier in the same chapter, Paul writes about learning the secret of being content in any and every situation, whether in plenty or in want (Philippians 4:12). His contentment is based on his confidence in God's faithfulness, knowing that God will meet his needs according to His riches in glory. This attitude of contentment underscores a key principle in Christian giving: while believers are called to support one another and the work of the ministry, the ultimate source of provision is God. Paul's reliance on God's provision serves as a model for both givers and receivers, reminding them that their trust should always be in God rather than in material resources.

Theological Implications of Supporting Ministry

"Moreover, as you Philippians know, in the early days of your acquaintance with the gospel, when I set out from Macedonia, not one church shared with me in the matter of giving and receiving, except you only; [16] for even when I was in Thessalonica, you sent me aid more than once when I was in need. [17] Not that I desire your gifts; what I desire is that more be credited to your account. [18] I have received full payment and have more than enough. I am amply supplied, now that I have received from Epaphroditus the gifts you sent. They are a fragrant offering, an acceptable sacrifice, pleasing to God". Philippians 4:15-18

Paul's words in Philippians 4:15-18 express important theological principles regarding the support of ministry in the early Church. The financial assistance provided by the Philippians signifies a partnership in the gospel. Their generosity allowed them to participate actively in Paul's ministry, contributing to the spread of the gospel. This partnership was not solely financial but spiritual, as they invested in the kingdom's work and shared its rewards. Paul's depiction of the Philippians' gifts as a "fragrant offering" and an "acceptable sacrifice" emphasizes that giving is an act of worship. It is a means for believers to honor God and contribute to His mission. This perspective elevates giving from a mere obligation to a sacred act that is pleasing to God.

Paul's emphasis on the spiritual benefits of giving implies that generosity holds eternal significance. Giving immediately supports a ministry, leading to long-term spiritual growth and rewards for faithful stewardship. Paul's contentment, despite relying on external support, serves as a reminder that God is the ultimate provider. This principle encourages givers and receivers to trust in God's provision, knowing He will meet their needs according to His will.

Philippians 4:15-18 illustrates how the early Church embraced and implemented financial support for ministry. The Philippians' generosity toward Paul went beyond a mere financial transaction; it embodied a partnership in the gospel, an act of worship, and a reflection of their deep commitment to God's mission. Their example challenges us to approach our giving with the same spirit of partnership, worship, and trust. When we support ministry work, we are not merely addressing practical needs; instead, we are actively contributing to spreading the gospel and offering a pleasing sacrifice to God. Our giving thus becomes a tangible expression of our faith, our dedication to God's purposes, and our trust in His provisions. Let us draw inspiration from the Philippians' example as we consider our financial support for the ministry, giving generously, willingly, and joyfully, knowing that our contributions bless others and honor God. In doing so, we carry forward the legacy of the early Church, furthering the kingdom's work and reaping the spiritual rewards of responsible stewardship.

Chapter 6

The Blessings of Tithing: Spiritual and Practical Benefits

"Trust in the Lord with all your heart and lean not on your own understanding; in all your ways submit to him, and he will make your paths straight." Proverbs 3:5-6

The Bible distinguishes between two types of blessings God bestows upon His people: spiritual and material. These blessings reflect God's goodness and care for His creation. Understanding the differences between spiritual and material blessings enables believers to appreciate God's provision more comprehensively, recognizing that God's blessings encompass more than just physical or financial prosperity. Spiritual blessings are intangible but powerful gifts that stem from a relationship with God through Jesus Christ. These eternal blessings are often associated with a believer's spiritual growth, inner transformation, and connection with God. Spiritual blessings encompass...

The most significant spiritual blessing is the gift of salvation through faith in Jesus Christ. According to Ephesians 2:8-9, "For it is b" grace you have been saved, through faith—and this is not from yourselves, it is the gift of God—not by works, so that no one can boast." This blessing assures eternal life and restores our relationship with God. Another profound spiritual blessing is the forgiveness of sins, made possible through Christ's sacrifice. 1 John 1:9 assures us, "If we confess our sins, he is faithful and just "and will forgive and purify us from all unrighteousness."

Upon salvation, believers receive the Holy Spirit, who dwells within them, guides them, and empowers them for godly living. Ephesians 1:13-14 describes the Holy Spirit as a 'seal' guaranteeing our inheritance as children of God. The blessings of peace and joy encompass the inner tranquility and happiness that stem from placing trust in God, irrespective of external circumstances. Philippians 4:7 assures, 'And the peace of God, which transcends all understanding, will guard your hearts and your minds in Christ Jesus, bringing a sense of joy and peace that surpasses all human understanding.'

Believers are bestowed with spiritual wisdom and guidance to confront life's trials. James 1:5 states, 'If any of you lacks wisdom, you should ask God, who gives generously to all without finding fault, and it will be given to you. This assurance of divine guidance and wisdom provides a strong sense of support and direction in life's challenges. Furthermore, spiritual blessings involve the journey of maturing in faith and striving to emulate Christ. Galatians 5:22-23 delineates the fruit of the Spirit—love, joy, peace, patience, kindness, goodness, faithfulness, gentleness, and self-control—as fundamental indicators of spiritual growth.

"Praise be to the God and Father of our Lord Jesus Christ, who has blessed us in the heavenly realms with every spiritual blessing in Christ.". Ephesians 1:3

Material blessings encompass the" various tangible, physical, and financial gifts believed to be provided by a higher power. These blessings can manifest as wealth, good health, possessions, food, shelter, and other resources that cater to our daily needs. It is a widely held belief that God promises to supply the basic material needs of His followers. According to Matthew (6:31-33", believers are urged not to fret over necessities such as food, drink, and clothing, but rather" to prioritize seeking God's kingdom and righteousness, with the assurance that all these needs will be fulfilled. Financial prosperity is often regarded" as a significant aspect of material blessings. In the book of Deuteronomy (28:12), material blessings are described as a part of God's covenants with Israel, with the promise that God will open the heavens to provide rain in due season and bless the work of their hands.

Health and "well-being are also considered part of material blessings. The book of 3 John (1:2) includes a prayer for material blessings," expressing the desire for good health and overall well-being. Furthermore, material blessings can extend to include success in work and business endeavors. Proverbs (3:9-10) encourages individuals to honor the Lord with their wealth and first fruits, with the promise that their storehouses will overflow, and their vault will be filled to the brim with new wine.

"God's promise t" Abraham encompasses both spiritual and material blessings. 'I will make you into a great nation and bless you; I will make your name great, and you will be a blessing. I will bless those who bless you, and whoever curses you I will curse, "and all peoples on earth will be blessed through you.'" - Genesis 12:2-3

Balancing Spiritual and Material Blessings

God bestows spiritual and material blessings, but the Bible emphasizes spiritual blessings more due to their eternal significance. Material blessings are transient, intended to provide for our needs and enable us to bless others, but they should not be the ultimate focus of our lives. Matthew 6:19-21 is advised, "Do not store up for yourselves treasures on earth, where moths and vermin destroy, and where thieves break in and steal. But store up for yourselves treasures in heaven… For where your treasure is, there your heart will be also."

The Bible warns against regarding material wealth as a sign of spiritual superiority or a guaranteed reward for faithfulness. 1 Timothy 6:9-10 cautions, "Those who want to get rich fall into temptation and a trap and into many foolish and harmful desires that plunge people into ruin and destruction. For the love of money is a root of all kinds of evil." Spiritual blessings, such as peace, joy, wisdom, and salvation, hold more value than material wealth. Jesus warned in Mark 8:36, "What good is it for someone to gain the whole world yet forfeit their soul?"

Pursuing spiritual blessings draws believers closer to God and cultivates qualities that transcend earthly life, offering a profound sense of purpose, tranquility, and satisfaction unmatched by material wealth. Romans 8:28 reassures believers that "in all things, God works for the good of those who love him," highlighting how spiritual blessings often emerge from adversity and prosperity as God molds us in the likeness of Christ.

Although fleeting, material blessings serve a vital role in God's realm. Followers are called to be responsible stewards of their material blessings and utilize them to aid others. 2 Corinthians 9:11 emphasizes, "You will be enriched in every way so that you can be generous on every occasion, and through us, your generosity will result in thanksgiving to God." Properly utilized, material blessings empower believers to support others and advance the work of God's kingdom.

Expressing gratitude for both spiritual and material blessings is essential. These blessings, both from God, serve distinct purposes in the lives of believers. Spiritual blessings are everlasting and nurture a deeper connection with God, while material blessings cater to our needs and provide us with the means to uplift others. Believers should prioritize spiritual blessings, trusting that God will meet their material needs as they walk in faith. Philippians 4:19 encapsulates this notion: "And my God will meet all your needs according to the riches of his glory in Christ Jesus."

Importance of Tithing

Tithing, giving one-tenth of one's income to support religious institutions or charitable causes, is a fundamental tenet in many faith traditions. This giving requires believers to trust God's provision, particularly when making a financial sacrifice. Tithing is not just a monetary contribution but an expression of faith and trust in God's ability to provide and sustain. By faithfully tithing, believers deepen their reliance on God, strengthening their faith and spiritual connection. This practice fosters a deeper understanding of the concept of stewardship. It cultivates a sense of gratitude for God's abundance, leading to a more profound spiritual growth and a closer relationship with God.

"Give, and it will be given to you. A good measure, pressed down, shaken together, and running over, will be poured into your lap. For with the measure you use, it will be measured to you." Luke 6:38

The practice of tithing plays a significant role in believers' spiritual growth. It requires regularity and commitment, which helps individuals develop spiritual discipline. This discipline is vital for overall spiritual development as it teaches believers to prioritize their relationship with God and consistently obey His commands. Moreover, tithing is a tangible reminder of a believer's faith in God. By choosing to give a portion of their income, individuals are prompted to look to God for their resources and to trust in God's ability to provide for their needs. This act of dependence fosters a deeper and more intimate relationship with God as believers learn to rely on Him for their daily sustenance.

Tithes encourages a shift in perspective towards a focus on eternal values rather than temporary gains by consistently giving to God's work; God learns to prioritize the advancement of God's kingdom over accumulating personal wealth. This encourages a mindset focused on impacting eternity and cultivates a kingdom-minded perspective among believers. Tithing is a divine invitation to deepen one's relationship with God. It is more than a simple financial transaction; it is a spiritual discipline that unveils the path to divine blessings and personal spiritual development.

Spiritual Benefits of Tithing

"Bring the whole tithe into the storehouse, that there may be food in my house. Test me in this," says the Lord Almighty, "and see if I will not throw open the floodgates of heaven and pour out so much blessing that there will not be room enough to store it." Malachi 3:10

Strengthening Faith and Trust in God: Tithing is a biblical practice that calls on believers to entrust God with their finances, particularly during challenging times. It involves giving a portion, typically ten percent, of one's income to God. By consistently offering this first portion to God, believers demonstrate and fortify their faith, relying on God to meet their needs. This act of faith serves as both a spiritual discipline and a tangible expression of confidence in God's provision. Malachi 3:10 underscores this by encouraging believers to "test" God and witness His faithfulness in response to their obedience. Tithing is a potent act of faith, even in financial hardship. Through their decision to give, believers affirm their trust in God's provision and discover a profound sense of security in His faithfulness. This practice strengthens their faith and fosters a deeper connection with Him, offering solace in uncertain times.

As faithful believers consistently tithe, they often witness unexpected and miraculous provisions from God in their lives. This may come as a sudden job opportunity, a financial windfall, or an expense reduction. These experiences strengthen their belief in God as a faithful provider and deepen their relationship with Him. The promise in Malachi 3:10-12 to "open the floodgates of heaven" and prevent loss demonstrates God's commitment to rewarding those who honor Him with their wealth.

"Test me in this," says the Lord Almighty, "and see if I will not throw open the floodgates of heaven and pour out so much blessing..." Malachi 3:10

Deepening Spiritual Maturity: Tithing catalyzes believers to prioritize God in their finances, contributing to the development of spiritual maturity. It requires discipline and a readiness to place God's kingdom first, even above personal financial security. Over time, this practice nurtures a more substantial reliance on God and a more pronounced focus on eternal values rather than fleeting material concerns, which are temporary and often distract from spiritual growth. Tithing fosters spiritual discipline and growth, guiding believers to prioritize God in their financial choices and to live with an eternal perspective, highlighting spiritual values over material wealth.

Tithing is an act of faith that demonstrates a believer's trust in God's provision, especially during financial uncertainty. When believers give, they put their faith into action, trusting that God will provide for their needs. This principle is encapsulated in Luke 6:38, which promises that those who give will receive in return. This assurance strengthens a believer's faith, reinforcing that God is faithful and generous. Tithing requires believers to trust God's provision, challenging them to entrust their finances to God, especially during uncertain times. By giving generously, believers affirm their trust that God will provide for their needs, even as they offer a portion of their income. This act of trust is a powerful means to bolster one's faith and opens the door for God to work more profoundly in their lives. Paul assures the Corinthians that God can bless them abundantly, ensuring they have everything they need to continue doing good, reinforcing the idea that tithing is an act of faith that deepens a believer's reliance on God.

Regular tithing is a transformative practice that encourages believers to cultivate a spirit of generosity. By giving, they exemplify God's generosity and, in turn, experience profound joy and fulfillment. The assurance that "with the measure you use, it will be measured to you" motivates believers to give generously, knowing that their generosity will be met with abundant blessings from God, uplifting their spirits. It is not merely a financial commitment but a spiritual discipline that promotes growth and self-control. Through consistent practice, tithing empowers believers to prioritize God in all aspects of life. It fosters spiritual maturity and a disciplined approach to living out their faith, giving them a sense of achievement and empowerment.

> *"Then all the nations will call you blessed, for yours will be a delightful land," says the Lord Almighty." Malachi 3:12*

Cultivating a Heart of Gratitude and Joy: Tithing encourages gratitude as believers acknowledge that everything they have comes from God. This gratitude naturally leads to joy, as believers find fulfillment in giving and witnessing the positive impact of their generosity on others. Paul's assurance that their generosity will result in thanksgiving to God underscores the joy and satisfaction of participating in God's work through giving.

Aligning with God's Will and Priorities: Tithing is an act of obedience and a means of spiritual growth that aligns believers with God's priorities. By giving the 'first fruits' of their income, believers prioritize God, indicating that His kingdom and righteousness are their foremost concerns. The concept of 'first fruits' refers to giving the best and first portion of one's income to God, symbolizing trust in His provision and acknowledging His sovereignty over all aspects of life. This alignment with God's will brings clarity and purpose to a believer's life, guiding them to live in a manner that honors God.

Cultivating a Heart of Generosity: Tithing fosters a spirit of generosity. By consistently giving, believers become more sensitive to the needs of others and more willing to share their blessings. This spirit of generosity reflects God's nature, and as believers practice it, they become more like Christ. Through tithing, believers tangibly experience God's grace. As they give, they become more aware of how much they have received from God and are moved to give freely, just as God gives to them. This experience of God's generosity inspires believers to be generous in return, creating a 'cycle of grace' where God's grace motivates believers to be gracious, and their generosity leads to more grace, blessing both the giver and the receiver.

Experiencing God's Faithfulness: Through tithing, believers can directly experience God's faithfulness. By giving, they frequently witness how God unexpectedly meets their needs, strengthening their trust in God as a reliable provider. Tithing promotes spiritual discipline and growth. It teaches believers to prioritize God in their financial decisions and to live with an eternal perspective, emphasizing spiritual values over material wealth.

Material Benefits of Tithing

"I will throw open the floodgates of heaven and pour out so much blessing that there will not be room enough to store it."
Malachi 3:10

"Bring the entire tithe into the storehouse so that there will be food in my house. Test me in this," says the Lord Almighty, "and see if I will not open the floodgates of heaven and pour out so many blessings that there will not be enough room to store them. I will prevent pests from devouring your crops, and the vines in your fields will not drop their fruit before it is ripe," says the Lord Almighty. "Then all the nations will call you blessed, for yours will be a delightful land," says the Lord Almighty."

> *"On the first day of every week, each one of you should set aside a sum of money in keeping with your income..." 1 Corinthians 16:2*

This excerpt embodies the principle of reciprocity between giving and receiving blessings, a fundamental concept in tithing. It urges followers to have faith in God's provision and consistently contribute to their spiritual community. The passage stresses that God's blessings are contingent upon faithfulness in tithing, which involves giving a tenth of one's income. It reassures believers of God's faithfulness by pledging that those who tithe will encounter His bountiful provision. The passage outlines the benefits of this practice as follows:

Abundant Provision: God's promise to "throw open the floodgates of heaven" suggests that those who tithe faithfully will receive prosperity in various ways. These could be monetary blessings, but they may also manifest as opportunities, personal growth, or other non-material successes.

Protection from Harm: God's assurance of preventing pests from devouring crops and ensuring vineyards produce fruit reminds us that those who use their resources to advance His works will be blessed with protection and stability in their livelihood and endeavors. Tithing is linked with God's promise of safeguarding a believer's resources. As believers give faithfully, God pledges to avert loss and bless their efforts, symbolized by the protection of crops in Malachi.

Recognition and Respect: Faithfulness in tithing leads to a reputation of being blessed and prosperous. Others will see the evidence of God's provision, bringing honor and recognition.

"I will prevent pests from devouring your crops, and the vines in your fields will not drop their fruit before it is ripe," says the Lord Almighty." Malachi 3:11

Experiencing Overflow and Generosity

Tithing is a practice through which believers receive God's blessings, often leading to abundance that allows them to meet their needs and support others. This creates a cycle of generosity, where blessings are shared, and God's work is furthered. Tithing is not just about fulfilling a religious obligation; it operates under the biblical principle of giving and receiving. It is a spiritual act that invites blessings into a believer's life, aligning with the broader biblical principle of generosity. Tithing is more than a financial transaction; it is a spiritual discipline that nurtures a generous spirit, encouraging believers to give regularly and sacrificially, reflecting God's character and aligning their hearts with His.

Developing Spiritual Discipline

"Honor the Lord with your wealth, with the first fruits of all your crops; then your barns will overflow, and your vats will brim over with new wine." Proverbs 3:9-10

Tithing is a financial act and a spiritual discipline that helps believers prioritize God in their lives. This discipline fosters spiritual growth and a more structured approach to living out one's faith. The 'good measure' overflowing symbolizes the abundance that God can bestow in response to tithing. This overflow encompasses material wealth, opportunities, peace, and joy. Luke 6:38 affirms that those who give will receive abundantly, suggesting that tithing can lead to material blessings as God honors the generosity of faithful givers. Honoring God with wealth is linked to the promise of material abundance in Proverbs 3:9-10. While this does not guarantee wealth, it does illustrate that God blesses those who give faithfully. These blessings may manifest as financial provisions, opportunities, or the joy and fulfillment of obeying God's commands.

> **"Give, and it will be given to you. A good measure, pressed down, shaken together, and running over, will be poured into your lap." Luke 6:38**

Understanding the Blessings of Tithing: Tithing is an act of giving and a means of receiving divine protection and favor. Malachi 3:10-11 assures that those who faithfully tithe will be provided for and protected by God. This divine safeguarding may manifest as the preservation of resources, success in business endeavors, or a sense of peace during challenging times. It is a powerful reminder that God always watches over us, ensuring that our needs are met and our resources are utilized for His glory. This promise of divine protection brings a deep sense of security and peace, knowing God is always there to watch over us.

Divine Protection for Resources: Malachi 3:11 promises divine protection for the resources of those who tithe. In ancient times, this protection was understood as guarding against pests and ensuring a fruitful harvest. For present-day believers, this translates to safeguarding their finances, careers, and other means of sustenance. God's protection ensures that the resources entrusted to believers are used effectively for His purposes and shielded from waste or destruction. Tithing is intricately linked to God's promise of safeguarding a believer's resources. Malachi 3:11 illustrates this by pledging protection from pests and guaranteeing the productivity of the land. For modern believers, God watches over their finances, investments, and other resources, ensuring that what remains after tithing is blessed and protected.

God's Abundant Provision: Luke 6:38 promises abundant provision to those who give. This principle suggests that tithing can lead to material blessings, as God rewards the generosity of faithful givers. The imagery of a 'good measure, pressed down, shaken together and running over' illustrates the overflowing nature of God's blessings. The promise in Malachi 3:10 that God will 'pour out so much blessing that there will not be room enough to store it' emphasizes the material benefits of tithing. While this doesn't necessarily mean financial wealth, it does indicate that God abundantly provides for those who are faithful in their giving. This provision can manifest in various forms, including economic stability, opportunities, and unexpected blessings.

Experiencing Overflow and Prosperity: The "good measure" that runs over signifies more than sufficiency—it speaks of abundance. Believers who tithe often discover that their needs are met and exceeded. This overflow may come in various forms, including financial prosperity, peace, opportunities, and joy. Tithing is not just about giving; it's about receiving God's abundant provision and experiencing a life of wealth and fulfillment. This overflow of blessings brings joy and a sense of satisfaction, knowing that God's provision is plentiful and consistently exceeds our needs.

Experiencing Overflow and Generosity: Those who practice tithing often discover themselves blessed with abundance, enabling them to support God's work and generously assist those in need. This overflow nurtures a culture of generosity, where God's blessings are multiplied and shared within the community of believers. Paul emphasizes that God can always bless believers with what they need. This promise of provision is a crucial material benefit of tithing. As believers give, they can trust that God will supply their needs, often in ways that exceed their expectations. This abundant provision is not just for personal gain but also to enable believers to continue doing good works. This sense of community and shared blessings makes believers feel connected and part of a larger purpose, knowing that their generosity is making a difference in the lives of others.

Tithing can lead to the multiplication of resources, with God increasing what the believer has sown. Paul's analogy of God supplying "seed to the Sower" suggests that as believers give, God will not only replenish what they have given but also increase their capacity to provide even more. This principle of multiplication, where God's grace ensures that those who give generously will always have the means to continue being generous, provides a sense of security and confidence in the believer's giving.

Tithing often sets off a cycle of generosity. As a person gives, they can receive even more blessings from God, allowing them to provide even more. This cycle of giving and receiving benefits the individual and the community by sharing resources and meeting needs. The blessings received through tithing enable believers to be generous in all circumstances. This ongoing generosity not only meets the needs of others but also amplifies the impact of the believer's giving, resulting in more abundant thanksgiving and glory to God. Consistent and generous giving through tithing yields significant material benefits, empowering believers to make a lasting and meaningful difference in the lives of others, reinforcing their sense of purpose and impact in their community.

Tithing as a Pathway to Spiritual Growth

Tithing offers a multitude of blessings, encompassing both spiritual and material rewards. The principle of generous giving, as outlined in 2 Corinthians 9:8-11, emphasizes the reciprocal relationship between giving and receiving in the Christian journey. Those who incorporate tithing as a regular practice will discover that it fortifies their faith, unlocks the gateway to God's bountiful provision, and enriches their spiritual development. Tithing transcends mere financial duty; it is a potent instrument for spiritual metamorphosis and a pathway to encounter God's abundant generosity.

Developing a Heart of Gratitude

Regular tithing helps believers cultivate gratitude by serving as a continual reminder of God's provision. They acknowledge that everything they have comes from God each time they give. This gratitude fosters a deeper connection with God, enhancing their spiritual life and creating greater contentment and joy. Embracing the fullness of tithing's blessings, including both spiritual and material benefits, encourages believers to adopt this practice as a means of deepening their faith and experiencing God's abundant blessings. It's important to emphasize that tithing is a holistic practice that brings about spiritual growth and tangible blessings, making it a vital component of a life that obeys God.

Tithing offers believers spiritual and material benefits, inspiring them to adopt this practice to strengthen their faith and receive abundant blessings from God. It is essential to highlight that tithing encompasses both spiritual growth and tangible blessings, making it a necessary aspect of life in obedience to God. By emphasizing the dual benefits of spiritual and material tithing, believers are encouraged to embrace it as a comprehensive practice that brings them closer to God and allows them to receive His blessings. It's crucial to underscore that the principle of giving and receiving forms a divine cycle that enriches the lives of those who faithfully participate.

Deepening a Relationship with God

"Come near to God, and he will come near you." James 4:8

Tithing is a means of drawing nearer to God. By consistently recognizing God's authority over their finances, believers strengthen their connection with Him. This practice cultivates intimacy with God as they encounter His faithfulness and provision in a personal and concrete manner. Through regular tithing, believers grow closer to God by acknowledging His sovereignty over their lives and finances. This practice fosters a deeper, more intimate relationship with God.

"Eat the tithe of your grain, new wine, and olive oil, and the firstborn of your herds and flocks in the presence of the Lord your God at the place he will choose as a dwelling for his

Name, so that you may learn to revere the Lord your God always." Deuteronomy 14:23

Tithing is a critical practice that involves regularly giving a portion of one's income to support religious or charitable causes. This regular commitment helps believers develop spiritual discipline and a deeper connection to their faith. By consistently setting aside a portion of their income for tithing, individuals can prioritize their relationship with God and demonstrate obedience to His commands. This discipline extends beyond just financial aspects and influences other areas of spiritual growth, promoting a life of consistent obedience to God's will. Tithing becomes a symbol of faith and a way to actively participate in one's religious community, fostering a sense of responsibility and commitment to the teachings of the faith. Ultimately, the regular practice of tithing can lead to a more disciplined and obedient lifestyle, impacting various aspects of a believer's life.

"Do not store up for yourselves treasures on earth, where moths and vermin destroy, and where thieves break in and steal. But store up for yourselves treasures in heaven..."
Matthew 6:19-20

As believers, we are called to invest in God's kingdom, shifting our focus from pursuing earthly wealth to laying up eternal treasures. This kingdom-focused perspective should shape our priorities and deepen our commitment to God's work. Tithing is a practical way to shift our focus from accumulating wealth on earth to investing in God's kingdom. When we regularly give a portion of our income to support God's work, we actively learn to prioritize eternal values over temporary material gains. This kingdom-minded perspective helps us commit more profoundly to God's purposes and align our lives more closely with His will.

Tithing requires believers to trust that God will provide for their needs, especially when they give generously. This reliance on God deepens our faith as we witness His faithfulness in response to our giving. Giving sacrificially demonstrates our trust in God's provision and sovereignty over our lives.

"And God can bless you abundantly, so that in all things at all times, having all that you need, you will abound in every good work." 2 Corinthians 9:8

Consistently tithing, individuals strengthen their connection with God as they consistently recognize His authority over their financial resources. This habit nurtures a more profound and intimate bond with God, defined by confidence and dependence.

"Come near to God, and he will come near to you." James 4:8

Discipline and Obedience

Tithing necessitates consistency and commitment, fostering spiritual discipline, and is essential for spiritual growth. It instructs believers to prioritize God's commands and obey His will. Regular tithing also extends to other areas of life, promoting a more disciplined and obedient lifestyle.

Tithing brings a multitude of blessings, both spiritual and material. The principle of giving and receiving, as outlined in Luke 6:38, underscores the reciprocal relationship between generosity and God's blessings. Believers who adopt tithing as a routine practice will discover that it fortifies their faith, unlocks God's abundant provision, and deepens their spiritual growth. Tithing transcends mere financial contributions and becomes a spiritual discipline in a believer's life.

"Eat the tithe of your grain, new wine, and olive oil, and the firstborn of your herds and flocks in the presence of the Lord your God at the place he will choose as a dwelling for his Name, so that you may learn to revere the Lord your God always." Deuteronomy 14:23

Encouraging a Kingdom-Minded Perspective

When believers practice tithing, they deliberately invest in God's kingdom. This act represents a conscious shift in focus from accumulating earthly wealth to seeking eternal treasures. By adopting a kingdom-minded perspective, individuals reorient their priorities and strengthen their dedication to advancing God's work.

"Do not store up for yourselves treasures on earth… But store up for yourselves treasures in heaven…" Matthew 6:19-20

Shifting Focus to Eternal Values

"Do not store up for yourselves treasures on earth… But store up for yourselves treasures in heaven… Matthew 6:19-20

Tithing reminds believers to invest in God's kingdom rather than earthly wealth. This shift in focus encourages prioritizing eternal values and storing treasures in heaven instead of accumulating temporary riches on earth. Such a kingdom-minded perspective is vital for spiritual growth as it aligns the believer's priorities with God's will.

Moreover, tithing helps believers to emphasize eternal rather than temporal values, fostering a kingdom mindset. It emphasizes the importance of storing treasures in heaven rather than accumulating wealth on earth.

As believers faithfully tithe, they cultivate contentment with what they have, trusting that God will meet their needs. This contentment fosters gratitude, which is an essential aspect of spiritual growth. Regular tithing instills contentment, leading to appreciation, which is crucial for spiritual growth. Expressing thankfulness for God's provision leads to a more profound sense of peace and joy in their spiritual journey.

> *"But godliness with contentment is great gain." 1 Timothy 6:6*

God's Grace and Generosity

As believers generously give of their time, talents, and resources, they deeply experience God's grace, coming to a profound realization that all blessings and gifts stem from Him. This heightened awareness fosters a stronger and more intimate connection to God's boundless generosity, inspiring and empowering believers to emulate this generosity in their own lives and spread kindness, love, and care to others.

> *"As it is written: 'They have freely scattered their gifts to the poor; their righteousness endures forever.'" 2 Corinthians 9:9*

Blessings of Generous Giving

Tithing is giving a portion of your income to the church or charitable causes, and it is often viewed as a generous act that aligns with God's will. It goes beyond just being a financial duty; tithing is a practice that is believed to open believers up to a multitude of blessings, both spiritual and material. Those who practice tithing often report experiencing blessings in various aspects of their lives, including improved financial situations, better health, and stronger relationships. These blessings enable believers to be generous on all occasions, not just when it comes to financial giving. Ultimately, the practice of tithing is believed to lead to a more significant impact on the lives of others and bring glory to God.

"You will be enriched in every way so that you can be generous on every occasion, and through us, your generosity will result in thanksgiving to God." 2 Corinthians 9:11

Heart of Gratitude and Joy

Regular tithing plays a crucial role in nurturing a heart of gratitude among believers. They consistently recognize and appreciate God's continuous provision and faithfulness in their lives. This intentional gratitude practice deepens their connection with God and enriches their spiritual journey.

As mentioned in Psalm 116:12, believers are prompted to reflect on what they can offer the Lord in response to His abundant goodness. Tithing serves as a tangible expression of this gratitude, encouraging believers to be thankful for what they have and experience the joy of giving to others. This mindset of gratitude contributes to a more joyful and content life, firmly grounded in the understanding that God's provision is abundant and unwavering.

"Now he who supplies seed to the sower and bread for food will also supply and increase your seed store and enlarge the harvest of your righteousness. You will be enriched in every

way so that you can be generous on every occasion, and through us, your generosity will result in thanksgiving to God." 2 Corinthians 9:10-11

God's Abundant Provision

God's promise to bless those who give generously is a powerful encouragement for believers. By giving generously, individuals invite God's provision into their lives, leading to an overflow of resources. This concept is beautifully captured in 2 Corinthians 9:8, which assures believers that God can bless them abundantly, ensuring they have all they need. This abundance enables believers to abound in every good work, reflecting the generosity and grace of God in their own lives.

The Multiplication of Resources

Tithing is a practice that involves giving a portion of one's income or resources, typically 10%, to support the work of the church or other charitable causes. It is believed that tithing can lead to a multiplication of resources, where God not only meets the giver's needs but also increases their ability to give even more. This principle of sowing and reaping ensures that generous givers are continually blessed with more to share. By faithfully giving, individuals can experience the joy of contributing to the well-being of others and witness the impact of their generosity in their own lives and the lives of those around them.

"He who supplies seed to the sower and bread for food will also supply and increase your store of seed and will enlarge the harvest of your righteousness." 2 Corinthians 9:10

Chapter 7

The Challenges of Tithing: Obstacles and Questions

"No one can serve two masters. Either you will hate the one and love the other, or you will be devoted to the one and despise the other. You cannot serve both God and money.

[25] *"Therefore I tell you, do not worry about your life, what you will eat or drink; or about your body, what you will wear. Is not life more than food, and the body more than clothes?* [26] *Look at the birds of the air; they do not sow or reap or store away in barns, and yet your heavenly Father feeds them. Are you not much more valuable than they?* [27] *Can any one of you by worrying add a single hour to your life[e]?*

[28] *"And why do you worry about clothes? See how the flowers of the field grow. They do not labor or spin.* [29] *Yet I tell you that not even Solomon in all his splendor was dressed like one of these.* [30] *If that is how God clothes the grass of the field, which is here today and tomorrow is thrown into the fire, will he not much more clothe you—you of little faith?* [31] *So do not worry, saying, 'What shall we eat?' or 'What shall we drink?' or 'What shall we wear?'* [32] *For the pagans run after all these things, and your heavenly Father knows that you need them.* [33] *But seek first his kingdom and his righteousness, and all these things will be given to you as well.* [34] *Therefore do not worry about tomorrow, for tomorrow will worry about itself. Each day has enough trouble of its own" Matthew 6:24-34*

Financial Difficulties and the Fear of Lack

It's a common struggle for many who practice tithing to balance their financial commitments. The weight of existing debt, low income, or unexpected expenses can make fulfilling this spiritual obligation challenging. The fear of financial insufficiency can lead to heightened anxiety and reluctance to contribute financially. Those who rely on their regular paychecks to cover their day-to-day expenses often find tithing an additional burden, making it challenging to prioritize and allocate funds accordingly.

Trusting God's Provision: In Matthew 6:24-34, Jesus addresses the fear of lack and emphasizes prioritizing trust in God over material concerns. He points out the impossibility of serving God and money, urging His followers to rely on God for their daily needs. By prioritizing the pursuit of God's kingdom, believers can find inspiration and freedom from anxiety about material provisions, trusting in God's promise to provide for them. In this context, tithing serves as an act of faith, demonstrating believers' confidence in God's ability to care for their needs.

Practical Steps for Managing Financial Stress: When encountering financial challenges, believers must approach the concept of tithing with careful consideration and wisdom. This may entail developing a detailed budget that includes provisions for giving, seeking out financial guidance from trusted sources, or initially starting with a smaller percentage and gradually increasing it as their faith and financial resources expand. The important thing is to take that initial step, feeling empowered that even the most minor acts of faith are honored by God.

The Necessity of Tithing

Some individuals who follow the Christian faith have expressed uncertainty regarding the continued relevance of tithing in the context of the New Testament. They perceive tithing as a practice from the Old Testament that may not directly apply to Christians today. This questioning has led to doubts about the obligation to tithe among some believers.

The New Testament introduces a shift in perspective regarding giving, explicitly moving away from the strict requirement of tithing and instead emphasizing the broader principle of generosity. Although the New Testament does not expressly mandate tithing, it consistently encourages believers to give, characterized by generosity and a cheerful attitude. Tithing serves as a foundational practice that promotes a lifestyle centered n generosity, effectively aligning with the overarching principles conveyed in the teachings of the New Testament.

Believers should have the freedom to choose whether to practice tithing to honor God and support the church while also understanding that they are not strictly bound by the Old Testament law. It is essential to emphasize giving joyfully and generously through tithing or other forms of financial support. This allows individuals to express their faith in a way that is meaningful to them while also contributing to the well-being of their religious community.

The Use of Tithes

Many individuals within the faith community may have differing views regarding allocating levies, which can hinder their generosity. Concerns may arise from the fear that their contributions are not being utilized prudently or that they are not making a tangible difference. Consequently, these apprehensions can result in individuals hesitating or feeling reluctant to fulfill their tithing commitments.

Churches must uphold accountability and stewardship when managing tithes. This involves providing regular, detailed financial reports to the congregation, maintaining clear communication regarding the allocation of funds, and demonstrating the tangible impact of church programs fueled by these contributions. When believers can see and understand how their donations are utilized effectively, it fosters a sense of confidence and trust in their giving.

Believers with questions or concerns about the allocation of tithes should be encouraged to actively participate in open dialogues and constructive discussions with church leadership. Fostering an environment of open communication can foster trust and accountability, ensuring that the church's financial resources are utilized in a manner consistent with its core mission and values.

Navigating the Challenges of Tithing with Faith

Tithing can be challenging for many people, but these challenges can be addressed with faith, wisdom, and open communication. It's essential to trust in God's provision when facing financial difficulties and to embrace the principle of generous giving. Additionally, seeking transparency in how tithes are used can help believers overcome obstacles to tithing. Ultimately, tithing is not just about giving money. It's an opportunity to grow in faith, experience God's blessings, and contribute to the work of the kingdom, enriching our spiritual journey and deepening our connection to our faith.

The Reality of Tithing Challenges

Tithing is a practice rooted in biblical teachings that can bring numerous benefits to believers. However, it's important to recognize that it can also pose real challenges for individuals. It's crucial to address these challenges openly and with compassion to assist believers in managing their financial and spiritual anxieties effectively.

Financial Difficulties and the Fear of Scarcity

Many individuals who adhere to a particular faith encounter financial challenges that make it difficult for them to tithe. These challenges may stem from indebtedness, low income, or unforeseen expenses, which can create anxiety and reluctance to contribute financially. This fear of scarcity often leads believers to prioritize their immediate financial needs over trusting a higher power to provide for them.

The concept of contentment plays a crucial role in fostering financial faithfulness, as highlighted in 1 Timothy 6:6-8. This passage emphasizes that godliness combined with contentment leads to significant gain. Cultivating a sense of contentment is essential for overcoming the fear of scarcity. When individuals are content with what they have, they are less likely to be consumed by financial anxieties and become more inclined to place their trust in a higher power about their financial resources. Contentment enables believers to direct their focus toward their spiritual development and reliance on their faith, bringing a sense of peace and reducing financial stress.

Practical Steps for Managing Financial Stress

When individuals who hold religious beliefs encounter financial difficulties, it can be helpful for them to take pragmatic measures to alleviate the stress. This may involve creating a detailed budget that accounts for income and expenses, prioritizing essential needs such as housing, food, and healthcare, and seeking guidance from financial counselors or advisors. Additionally, for believers who wish to practice tithing, it's important to remember that it's okay to start with a smaller percentage of giving and gradually increase the amount as their financial situation improves. This approach can allow individuals to uphold their religious commitments without feeling overwhelmed by financial strain, providing a sense of comfort and reassurance.

The Dangers of Loving Money and Materialism

Understanding the Challenge: The love of money and materialism can present significant barriers to tithing, the practice of giving a portion of one's income to support religious or charitable causes. In our culture, there is often an emphasis on equating success with wealth, which can lead believers to struggle with the temptation to prioritize financial gain over spiritual growth. This struggle can result in a mindset where tithing is viewed as a loss of money rather than a meaningful act of worship and generosity.

The Bible passage in 1 Timothy 6:9-10 cautions believers about the perils of being consumed by the love of money. It emphasizes that such an obsession can result in harmful behaviors and spiritual deterioration. The relentless pursuit of wealth can ensnare individuals, leading them into temptation and causing them to neglect their spiritual connection with God. Tithing is a solution to counteract the grip of materialism on a believer's life, redirecting their focus towards the kingdom of God and eternal principles.

Cultivating a Spirit of Generosity: To counteract the adverse effects of the love of money, believers are encouraged to cultivate a spirit of generosity actively. This involves not only giving financially but also giving of one's time, talents, and resources. Tithing is highlighted as a practical way to develop this spirit of generosity, as it teaches believers to give joyfully and prioritize God's work over accumulating wealth. By embracing tithing and generosity, believers shift their perspective from material wealth to spiritual fulfillment, finding joy and purpose in giving rather than acquiring more possessions. This change in mindset leads to a more profound sense of contentment and satisfaction in life.

The Use of Tithes

Understanding the Concern: Many individuals have expressed concerns about how their tithes are utilized, leading to hesitation in their giving. Believers need to clearly understand the transparency, accountability, and effectiveness of their contributions. Without this clarity, they may question whether their tithes genuinely make a meaningful difference in the causes they support.

Promoting Accountability and Stewardship: Churches must uphold a high standard of transparency and responsibility in managing tithes. This involves providing detailed and easily accessible information about the allocation of funds, conducting regular and comprehensive financial reporting, and clearly illustrating the tangible impact of church programs on the community and congregation. By consistently demonstrating prudent stewardship practices, churches can establish and reinforce trust with their members, thus fostering a culture of sustained and meaningful financial support.

When considering levies, believers are encouraged to engage in open and transparent dialogue with church leadership. These conversations can offer valuable insights and reassurance, allowing believers to understand how their tithes are being utilized to advance God's work. Moreover, individuals may support ministries or missions that resonate with their values and interests, ensuring that their contributions are channeled toward causes that deeply matter to them.

Overcoming: Challenges with Faith and Wisdom

Overcoming the challenges of tithing requires a foundation of faith, contentment, and wise decision-making. By leaning on God's provision, resisting the lure of material wealth, and actively engaging in the church's life, believers can effectively navigate the obstacles associated with tithing. This wise decision-making empowers believers, ultimately presenting an opportunity for personal growth in faith, nurturing a generous spirit, and contributing meaningfully to advancing God's kingdom.

Financial Difficulties and the Fear of Scarcity

Financial challenges pose a significant barrier for many individuals regarding tithing. The worry of insufficient funds can make giving 10% of one's income seem daunting, especially in circumstances such as job loss, increasing debt, or a low income. This apprehension often results in anxiety and hesitancy to levy, as individuals may prioritize addressing their immediate financial requirements over honoring their commitment to giving.

In Matthew 6:24-34, Jesus emphasizes the importance of not letting worry over material needs consume believers. He draws a clear contrast between serving God and serving money, urging His followers to prioritize seeking God's kingdom and trusting God to provide for their needs. This passage underscores the significance of tithing as an act of faith, demonstrating trust in God's provision even when finances are tight. By placing God's kingdom first, believers open themselves to receiving His provision, reinforcing the belief that tithing is not just a financial obligation, but a testament of faith.

Managing Financial Stress: When dealing with financial difficulties, it's important to balance faith and practicality when addressing the practice of tithing. Practical steps such as developing a detailed budget, identifying, and eliminating unnecessary expenses, and seeking guidance from financial experts can effectively alleviate stress. Furthermore, individuals can start by contributing a smaller percentage of their income and gradually increase it as their financial situation improves. This approach not only makes the practice of tithing more manageable but also instills a sense of progress, encouraging believers to continue demonstrating generosity.

Doubts About the Necessity of Tithing

Understanding the Doubt: Some believers question whether tithing is still relevant or necessary under the new covenant. They may see it as an Old Testament practice that doesn't apply to Christians today, leading to uncertainty about whether they should tithe.

Jesus' Teaching on Generosity: Jesus emphasizes the importance of generosity and giving from the heart rather than out of obligation. While tithing is not explicitly commanded in the New Testament, the principle of generous giving remains central to Christian practice. Luke 6:38 encourages believers to give generously, promising they will receive in return. Tithing can be viewed as a foundational practice that helps cultivate a spirit of generosity.

Embracing the Principle of Generosity: Rather than viewing tithing as a strict requirement, believers can embrace it as a valuable practice that aligns with the broader biblical principle of generosity. Tithing is a way to express gratitude to God and support His work, reflecting a heart aligned with His purposes.

Concerns About How Tithes Are Used

Concerns about the use of levies can lead to hesitation in giving. Believers may worry about whether their contributions are being used effectively and with integrity. Issues such as a lack of transparency in how the funds are managed, poor financial management practices, or misuse of funds can cause distrust and reluctance to tithe. This lack of trust can impact individuals' willingness to contribute to their religious organizations, potentially hindering the community's financial stability and outreach efforts.

Importance of Trust and Transparency: Churches must prioritize trust and transparency in their financial management. This involves consistently providing detailed financial reports to the congregation, openly communicating how funds are allocated and utilized, and demonstrating a solid dedication to responsible stewardship. Building and maintaining trust with the congregation is contingent upon demonstrating wise and impactful management of tithes, as this fosters confidence and encourages continued giving.

When believers have concerns about allocating their tithes, they must feel empowered to have open and transparent discussions with church leadership. This can include requesting detailed financial reports, actively participating in budget meetings, or expressing support for specific ministries. By engaging in these ways, believers can gain a deeper understanding of how their contributions are utilized, which fosters a greater sense of ownership and trust in the church's financial stewardship.

Financial Difficulties and the Fear of Insufficiency

Many individuals who adhere to tithing encounter challenges due to financial hardships. Concerns stemming from debt, insufficient income, and unforeseen expenses often create significant barriers to giving 10% of one's earnings. The fear of experiencing scarcity can trigger feelings of anxiety and reluctance to engage in tithing practices.

In Matthew 23:23, Jesus admonishes the Pharisees, pointing out their meticulous observance of tithing while neglecting weightier matters such as justice, mercy, and faithfulness. This passage serves as a potent reminder that while tithing is important, it should not overshadow the significance of other essential aspects of life. It underscores the need for believers to strike a balance between demonstrating faith through tithing and exercising prudence in managing their financial resources. It encourages individuals to trust God's provision while being responsible stewards of their finances, ensuring spiritual and economic well-being and empowering them to take control of their financial situation.

When dealing with financial challenges, it is crucial to address the practice of tithing with a blend of faith and prudence. Implementing practical approaches such as creating a detailed budget, identifying, and prioritizing essential expenses (e.g., housing, food, utilities), and seeking professional guidance can alleviate financial strain. It may be beneficial to commence tithing with a modest percentage and incrementally raise the contribution as financial security strengthens, thereby making the practice more sustainable.

Doubts About the Necessity of Tithing

Some believers have raised doubts about the necessity and relevance of tithing in the New Testament era. They question whether tithing, often considered an Old Testament practice, applies to Christians today.

In Matthew 23:23, Jesus upholds the importance of tithing while stressing the need for a balanced approach that incorporates justice, mercy, and faithfulness. This passage suggests that tithing should not be divorced from the broader principles of love and justice that Jesus espoused. Rather than being a legalistic requirement, tithing should be embraced as part of a holistic approach to generosity and righteousness, reflecting a heart attuned to love and justice.

Furthermore, believers are encouraged to view tithing as a meaningful practice that nurtures a spirit of generosity. Rather than simply fulfilling an obligation, tithing can be seen as a foundational step towards cultivating a generous heart. It is a starting point for a life characterized by selfless giving, driven by love and gratitude rather than mere duty.

Questions About the Use of Tithes

Many individuals may need help contributing tithes due to concerns regarding how their donations are utilized. They may worry about the lack of transparency and accountability in their church's financial management and doubt the efficacy of their contributions.

The Importance of Justice and Stewardship: Just as Jesus criticized the Pharisees for neglecting justice while tithing, churches must ensure that tithes are used responsibly and justly. This includes supporting the needy by providing food, shelter, and other essential support, funding meaningful ministry work such as outreach programs, missionary efforts, and community development projects, and maintaining transparency in financial practices by regularly publishing detailed financial reports and budgets. Churches that practice good stewardship build trust with their congregation, encouraging more consistent giving and allowing for greater impact in their communities."

Encouraging Involvement and Dialogue: Believers who have concerns about how their tithes are used must feel empowered to engage in open and transparent discussions with church leadership. By asking questions about the allocation of funds, participating in church budget planning meetings, or supporting specific ministries directly, believers can ensure that their financial contributions align with their values and the church's mission. This open dialogue and involvement can help create a sense of accountability and transparency within the church community regarding using funds.

The Potential for Legalism and Missing the Bigger Picture

Overemphasizing tithing while neglecting broader Christian responsibilities can lead to a legalistic approach. This approach, devoid of the fundamental essence of God's desires, may result in a shallow and incomplete understanding of Christian faith and practice.

Practicing holistic discipleship involves engaging in various Christian virtues, including tithing, justice, mercy, and faithfulness. Tithing, while essential, is not a standalone practice. It is part of a comprehensive lifestyle of faith, where believers follow Jesus in all areas of life, integrating tithing with other aspects of Christian discipleship.

A balanced approach to faith in the context of tithing is not about rules and obligations, but about freedom and grace. It involves integrating the act of giving into a life wholly dedicated to following Jesus' teachings. This holistic approach emphasizes the financial aspect of tithing and the principles of generosity, justice, and mercy. By prioritizing these values, believers can avoid the trap of legalism and ensure that their giving is a genuine reflection of a heart aligned with God's will.

The believers should know that Tithing may present challenges, but these obstacles can be navigated with wisdom, faith, and a balanced perspective. By trusting in God's provision, avoiding legalism, and striving to practice justice, mercy, and faithfulness, believers can overcome the hurdles associated with tithing. Ultimately, tithing is a crucial practice, forming part of a broader commitment to living out the Christian faith in a manner that honors God and reflects His love for others.

Financial Difficulties and the Fear of Insufficiency

Understanding the Challenge: Financial difficulties are one of the most common obstacles to tithing. Believers may need help with the idea of giving away a portion of their income when they are already dealing with debt, low income, or unexpected expenses. The fear of not having enough to meet their own needs can lead to anxiety and reluctance to tithe.

Faith in Action: Trusting God Amid Financial Struggles: James 2:14-17 emphasizes the importance of putting faith into action. Just as faith without works is dead, tithing is a practical way to demonstrate trust in God's provision. Even when finances are tight, tithing can be a step of faith that reflects a commitment to living out one's beliefs. By trusting God with their finances, believers can experience His faithfulness and provision in new and unexpected ways.

Financial Management: For those facing financial difficulties, it's essential to approach tithing with both faith and wisdom. Practical strategies like budgeting, prioritizing critical expenses, and seeking financial counseling can help manage financial stress. Starting with a smaller percentage and gradually increasing the levy as financial stability improves can make tithing more manageable while allowing believers to practice generosity.

The Necessity of Tithing

Dealing with Uncertainty: Believers often wonder whether tithing is still necessary or relevant in the New Testament era. It's understandable to see it as an Old Testament practice that doesn't apply to Christians today, leading to uncertainty about whether they should tithe.

The Practicality of Tithing: James 2:14-17 teaches that genuine faith is demonstrated through actions. While the New Testament emphasizes generosity rather than a strict requirement to tithe, tithing can be seen as a practical expression of faith. It's a tangible way to support God's work, showing that believers trust God's provision and are committed to His kingdom.

Embracing a Lifestyle of Generosity: Instead of viewing tithing as a rigid requirement, believers can embrace it as part of a broader lifestyle of generosity. Tithing is a practical way to live out the principles of generosity that Jesus and the apostles taught, reflecting a heart aligned with God's purposes and committed to supporting the church's work. This act of giving creates a sense of community and unity among believers, making them feel connected and part of a larger purpose.

Many individuals may need to be more concerned about allocating levies, leading to a reluctance to contribute. Believers may be apprehensive about whether their donations are utilized responsibly and ethically, especially if they perceive a lack of transparency or accountability in their church's financial management. This apprehension can significantly impact their willingness to give.

Churches should prioritize faithful stewardship to maintain transparency and accountability in managing and utilizing tithes. This involves emphasizing the importance of practical deeds alongside faith, as James highlights, and implementing clear and open communication regarding the allocation and use of funds. Regular financial reporting is crucial in demonstrating responsible stewardship, and it is essential to ensure that levies are utilized to support meaningful and impactful ministry work. By practicing good stewardship and transparency, churches can establish and strengthen trust with their congregation, ultimately fostering more consistent and meaningful giving within the community.

Believers concerned about tithe use should feel empowered to engage in open discussions with church leadership. They can ask questions about budgeting, how funds are allocated to different ministries, and what specific initiatives are being supported. Additionally, believers can actively participate in church financial planning by offering their input on budget decisions and financial transparency. By supporting ministries, believers can ensure that their contributions are used effectively and aligned with their values. This involvement and dialogue can help foster a sense of transparency and accountability within the church community.

Balancing Faith, Deeds, and Legalism

Understanding the Risk: James cautions in his letter that focusing excessively on tithing as a legalistic obligation, which is a rigid adherence to the letter of the law rather than the spirit of it, can result in a faith that lacks vitality. When Tithing is carried out as a mere sense of duty rather than an authentic expression of faith and love, it can lose its spiritual significance and become a mere ritual.

Integrating Tithing into a Holistic Faith: Tithing should be seen as a vital part of a comprehensive approach to faith, where it is just one of the many ways believers demonstrate their commitment to God and His work. Tithing should be viewed as an integral part of a broader life of faith that encompasses justice, mercy, and love. By incorporating tithing into holistic discipleship, believers can steer clear of legalism and ensure that their giving reflects a heart aligned with God's will.

Striving for a Balanced View: Having a balanced perspective on Tithing means recognizing its significance as a spiritual practice and integrating it into the overall framework of Christian discipleship. Tithing holds meaning when approached with sincerity and complemented by other expressions of faith and service. Believers must maintain a well-rounded approach to their faith, where Tithing is just one aspect of their dedication to following Jesus.

Tithing comes with challenges; these can be managed through faith, practical wisdom, and a balanced mindset. By relying on God's provision, incorporating tithing into a comprehensive faith, and striving for transparency and accountability in tithes, believers can overcome the difficulties associated with Tithing. Ultimately, Tithing is a significant practice, but it's just a part of the broader commitment to living out the Christian faith in a way that glorifies God and embodies His love for others, a commitment that unites us all in our spiritual journey.

Chapter 8

Tithing vs. Grace Giving: A New Covenant Approach

"And now, brothers and sisters, we want you to know about the grace that God has given the Macedonian churches. [2] In the midst of a very severe trial, their overflowing joy and their extreme poverty welled up in rich generosity. [3] For I testify that they gave as much as they were able, and even beyond their ability. Entirely on their own, [4] they urgently pleaded with us for the privilege of sharing in this service to the Lord's people.[5] And they exceeded our expectations: They gave themselves first to the Lord, and then by the will of God also to us". 2 Corinthians 8:1-5

The Shift from Law to Grace

Tithing was essential for the Israelites to fulfill their religious duties and support the spiritual system. However, with the advent of Christ and the establishment of the New Covenant, the focus shifted from legal obligations to a life guided by grace and love. This transition is fundamental to understanding the distinction between tithing and grace-giving. Tithing was deeply ingrained in the Old Testament law, serving practical purposes such as supporting the Levitical priesthood and providing for the impoverished. However, as a legalistic practice, it often became more about meeting a requirement than expressing genuine devotion. The limitations of this approach became apparent when tithing was carried out as an obligation rather than an act of worship. Grace-giving, on the other hand, is a voluntary, cheerful, and sacrificial act of giving, inspired by the grace we have received from God. It is not about meeting a quota, but about responding to God's love with a generous heart.

Tithing was significant in the Old Testament law, as it supported the Levitical priesthood and provided for those in need. The Levitical priesthood was a hereditary priesthood in ancient Israel, responsible for the religious rituals and ceremonies, as well as teaching and guiding the people in matters of faith and morality. However, over time, the original purpose of tithing became overshadowed by legalistic interpretations, leading to a focus on meeting a requirement rather than demonstrating sincere devotion. This shift revealed the limitations of an approach to tithing that prioritized obligation over genuine worship.

In the Old Testament, tithing was mandatory to sustain Israel's religious structure, typically giving 10% of one's income or agricultural yield. It played a crucial role in supporting the temple and the Levitical priesthood. With the advent of Christ and the institution of the New Covenant, followers are encouraged to embrace a more profound, grace-centered perspective on generosity that surpasses the legalistic demands of the Old Testament.

The encounter between Abraham and Melchizedek beautifully illustrates the significance of tithing. It portrays tithing as more than a mere obligation but an expression of reverence and adoration. Melchizedek, a king and a priest, foreshadows Christ's superior priesthood. When Abraham tithed to Melchizedek, it symbolized his acknowledgment of a higher spiritual authority.

In the New Covenant, Christ fulfills this role, and our giving becomes an act of honoring Him, transcending the mere legalistic practice of tithing. The churches in Macedonia serve as a profound example of grace-filled generosity. Despite facing financial hardships, the members of these churches wholeheartedly and cheerfully contributed, driven by the grace they had experienced from God. Their giving was not a result of obligation but stemmed from a profound sense of love and thankfulness. This compelling example beautifully embodies the essence of grace-giving, emphasizing that our giving, when rooted in grace, has the power to transform lives and communities, regardless of the amount given.

"Therefore, I urge you, brothers, and sisters, in view of God's mercy, to offer your bodies as a living sacrifice, holy and pleasing to God—this is your true and proper worship. ² Do not conform to the pattern of this world but be transformed by the renewing of your mind. Then you will be able to test and approve what God's will is—his good, pleasing, and perfect will". Romans 12:1-2

Grace Giving as a Way of Life

Romans 12:1-2 urges believers to present their lives as sacrifices to God, reshaping our understanding of worship and giving. Under the New Covenant, worship transcends legalistic requirements, encompassing all aspects of our lives, including our finances. This transformed approach to giving reflects a heart entirely devoted to God and committed to pleasing Him in every way.

Grace giving introduces a more profound and liberating form of generosity under the New Covenant, moving beyond the constraints of legalistic tithing. It encourages believers to give as worship, driven by love and gratitude for God's mercy. Embracing grace-giving transcends the fixed percentage of tithing. Instead, believers are called to give freely and generously, as they have decided. This approach underscores the freedom and responsibility that accompany grace. While there is no prescribed amount, believers are encouraged to give sacrificially and joyfully, reflecting the abundant love of Christ.

Grace giving is a transformative and empowering concept within the framework of the New Covenant. It represents a departure from the rigid and legalistic practice of tithing, instead encouraging believers to approach giving as a heartfelt expression of worship. Motivated by love and profound gratitude for Christ's sacrifice, grace-giving enables individuals to advance Christ's mission actively. It allows believers to authentically embody the freedom and generosity that stem from being integral members of His kingdom.

Freedom in Christ

"This Melchizedek was king of Salem and priest of God Most High. He met Abraham returning from the defeat of the kings and blessed him, [2] and Abraham gave him a tenth of everything. First, the name Melchizedek means "king of righteousness"; then also, "king of Salem" means "king of peace." [3] Without father or mother, without genealogy, without beginning of days or end of life, resembling the Son of God, he remains a priest forever. [4] Just think how great he was: Even the patriarch Abraham gave him a tenth of the plunder! [5] Now the law requires the descendants of Levi who become priests to collect a tenth from the people—that is, from their fellow Israelites—even though they also are descended from Abraham. [6] This man, however, did not trace his descent from Levi, yet he collected a tenth from Abraham and blessed him who had the promises. [7] And without doubt the lesser is blessed by the greater. [8] In the one case, the tenth is collected by people who die; but in the other case, by him who is declared to be living. [9] One might even say that Levi, who collects the tenth, paid the tenth through Abraham, [10] because when

Melchizedek met Abraham, Levi was still in the body of his ancestor". Hebrews 7:1-10,

In the Old Testament, tithing was a mandatory practice for the Israelites to fulfill their obligations to God and support the religious system. However, with the New Covenant, the emphasis shifts from fulfilling obligations to embracing the freedom provided by Christ. Galatians 5:1 emphasizes that Christ has liberated us from the burdens of the law, including the legalistic practice of tithing. This freedom allows believers to give generously, driven by love and gratitude rather than duty.

Galatians 5:1 teaches that believers are no longer bound by the legalistic requirements of the law, including tithing. Instead, they are encouraged to live in the freedom that Christ provides, giving as the Holy Spirit leads them. Grace giving is not about meeting a specific percentage but giving generously, motivated by love and gratitude for the grace believers have received from God. This approach to giving reflects the transformation that comes from living in the freedom of Christ.

In the New Covenant, believers are no longer bound by the law of tithing. Instead, they are called to give in response to the grace they have received through Christ, our High Priest, in the order of Melchizedek. Grace giving is characterized by generosity, love, and a desire to worship Christ through our resources. It is not about meeting a specific percentage but giving freely and sacrificially as the Spirit leads. Grace-giving transcends the fixed rate of tithing. Under the New Covenant, believers are called to give freely and generously, according to what they have decided in their hearts.

This approach emphasizes the freedom and responsibility that come with grace. While there is no set amount, believers are encouraged to give sacrificially and joyfully, reflecting the generous love of Christ. Grace giving surpasses the fixed 10% of tithing, inviting believers to give as the Holy Spirit leads, without the constraints of legalism. This freedom in Christ allows for more spontaneous and joyful giving, where believers are motivated by love and gratitude. Just as Abraham's tithe to Melchizedek was an act of worship, so is grace acknowledging Christ's lordship and participation in His mission. The personal decision in grace giving empowers believers and underscores their responsibility in managing the resources God has entrusted to them.

Living Out Grace Giving

Living out grace-giving involves

- Nurturing a generous heart.
- Aligning one's giving with God's kingdom purposes.
- Embracing the joy and blessings of giving.

Believers are encouraged to seek God's guidance in their giving, seek opportunities to offer beyond the tithe, and do so with a spirit of joy and gratitude. Grace-giving is not merely an obligation but a joyful response to the grace and mercy we have received in Christ. Believers are urged to seek God's guidance in their giving, to seek opportunities to give beyond the tithe actively, and to do so with a spirit of joy and gratitude, recognizing that their giving reflects their commitment to God.

Chapter 9

Is Tithing Necessary Today? Perspectives and Practices

"One person considers one day more sacred than another; another considers every day alike. Each of them should be fully convinced in their own mind. ⁶ Whoever regards one day as special does so to the Lord. Whoever eats meat does so to the Lord, for they give thanks to God; and whoever abstains does so to the Lord and gives thanks to God. ⁷ For none of us lives for ourselves alone, and none of us dies for ourselves alone. ⁸ If we live, we live for the Lord; and if we die, we die for the Lord. So, whether we live or die, we belong to the Lord." Romans 14:5-8

This chapter aims to provide a comprehensive analysis of various theological viewpoints on this topic and offer practical guidance for believers who are sincerely interested in understanding and implementing the concept of tithing in their daily lives. Drawing inspiration from the teachings in Romans 14:5-8, we will underscore the significance of personal convictions in matters of faith and how individuals can make well-informed and heartfelt decisions about their giving, ensuring that they do so with integrity and a clear conscience. This chapter will delve into the ongoing debate regarding the necessity of tithing in the contemporary church, specifically focusing on how tithing and other forms of giving contribute to ministry work. Building on the foundational text of 1 Corinthians 9:13-14, we aim to explore diverse theological perspectives on tithing and provide practical guidance for believers, equipping them to grasp and embrace the principle of tithing in today's context.

"Don't you know that those who serve in the temple get their food from the temple, and that those who serve at the altar share in what is offered on the altar? [14] *In the same way, the Lord has commanded that those who preach the gospel should receive their living from the gospel". 1 Corinthians 9:13-14.*

We shall also explore the ongoing discussion surrounding the relevance of tithing in today's church. By examining Colossians 3:17, we aim to understand how believers can approach tithing and giving within their commitment to do everything in the name of the Lord. This chapter will present diverse theological perspectives on tithing and provide practical guidance for believers seeking to comprehend and apply this principle in their lives today. Grounded in James 1:5, which urges believers to seek wisdom from God in decision-making, we will delve into various theological viewpoints on tithing. Furthermore, we will offer practical advice, emphasizing the significant reassurance and guidance that comes from seeking divine wisdom when making these decisions.

"And whatever you do, whether in word or deed, do it all in the name of the Lord Jesus, giving thanks to God the Father through him". Colossians 3:17

The Debate Over Tithing in the Modern Church

The ongoing debate regarding tithing reflects a larger theological question about applying Old Testament practices within the context of the New Covenant. There is a spectrum of beliefs among Christians regarding tithing, with some adherents considering it a continuing obligation. In contrast, others interpret it as a tradition fulfilled in Christ and, therefore, not mandatory for New Testament followers. In Romans 14:5-8, the apostle Paul emphasizes the importance of personal convictions, acknowledging that individual believers may hold differing perspectives. This chapter serves as a valuable guide for Christians, affirming the freedom of their beliefs as they seek to make moral decisions about tithing and other related practices, ensuring that they do so with integrity and a clear conscience.

What should I do if my beliefs about tithing are different from others? Differing beliefs about tithing can sometimes lead to tension within the Christian community. However, Romans 14 offers guidance on how to handle this situation. It encourages mutual respect and advises against passing judgment, emphasizing that each believer's conviction should be honored as a sincere expression of faith. This chapter in the Bible encourages Christians to uphold their own beliefs while respecting the beliefs of others, promoting unity and understanding within the community, and ensuring that everyone feels included and part of a harmonious community.

Believers often wrestle with the question of whether their contributions are sufficient. It's essential to shift the focus from the specific amount given to the spirit behind the giving. Rather than fixating on quantity, God places more excellent value on a willing and joyful heart. Believers are urged to give with gratitude, offering what they can with a spirit of thankfulness, knowing that God highly values their willingness and joy in giving.

Tithing is a concept that goes beyond monetary donations. It encompasses giving time, talents, and other resources. This holistic approach to stewardship and generosity encourages believers to offer all aspects of their lives as a form of giving to God. It's not just about financial contributions but also about investing time, sharing talents, and utilizing other resources to benefit the church and the community. Believers are urged to view tithing as a way to support the church's work and contribute to the betterment of the community in diverse and meaningful ways.

Fulfilling the practice of tithing can be challenging when facing financial difficulties. However, it's important to remember that God's wisdom encompasses understanding each individual's unique circumstances. Believers are encouraged to give by their financial means and to prioritize the intention and spirit of their giving rather than fixating on a specific monetary amount. While financial constraints may make tithing seem daunting, focusing on giving from the heart is essential. God values a willing and cheerful giver, regardless of the amount contributed.

When it comes to ensuring that our giving honors God, believers can take intentional and purposeful steps in their contributions. This involves carefully selecting ministries and causes that align with God's work and providing with the sincere desire to advance His kingdom. Seeking wisdom and guidance in choosing where and how to give is crucial in this process. Being intentional and purposeful ensures that our giving aligns with our spiritual values and priorities, allowing us to make a meaningful impact by God's will.

Personal Convictions in Matters of Faith

"Each of you should give what you have decided in your heart to give, not reluctantly or under compulsion, for God loves a cheerful giver." 2. The Role of Personal Convictions in Faith. 2 Corinthians 9:7

Personal convictions play a crucial role when Scripture does not provide a direct command, such as tithing under the New Covenant. Romans 14:5-8 offers wisdom on approaching such issues: "One person considers one day more sacred than another; another considers every day alike. They should be fully convinced in their mind… whether we live or die, we belong to the Lord." Paul emphasizes that, in non-essential matters of faith, believers are free to follow their convictions while maintaining unity and respect for others with different views. This freedom in personal convictions empowers believers, respecting their individual journey of faith. Applied to tithing, this means that some believers may feel called by sentence to continue the practice of tithing as a discipline that honors God. Others may give generously without adhering to a fixed percentage, believing grace-based giving reflects our freedom in Christ. Both approaches can be valid expressions of faith as long as they are done with the right heart and for the glory of God.

In addressing the ongoing debate over tithing, believers should recognize that God cares more about the heart behind giving than the specific method or percentage. The New Testament emphasizes generosity, grace, and the joy of giving, inviting believers to participate in God's work by supporting the church and caring for the needy. This emphasis on the joy of giving invokes a sense of fulfillment and happiness in the audience. Ultimately, the decision to tithe or give in another form should be driven by personal conviction and a desire to honor God. Whether or not tithing is necessary today, the generous, sacrificial giving principle remains central to Christian faith and practice. By focusing on the heart of giving, believers can move beyond legalistic debates and live out a faith that reflects God's grace and goodness.

Generosity Over Obligation

The New Testament emphasizes that giving should stem from a transformed heart rather than obligation. In 1 Corinthians 16:1-2, Paul offers practical advice on sharing: "Now about the collection for the Lord's people... On the first day of every week, you should set aside a sum of money in keeping with your income." This passage encourages regular, intentional giving without enforcing a strict percentage, emphasizing proportionate giving reflective of the spirit of generosity rather than the letter of the law. The focus is on the giver's heart. Proverbs 3:9-10 encourages believers to "Honor the Lord with your wealth, with the first fruits of all your crops." This principle of honoring God with the best of what we have remains relevant today, whether through tithing or sacrificial giving exceeding 10%. Balancing Generosity with Financial Stewardship: Offer practical steps for balancing generosity with responsible financial stewardship. Believers are encouraged to budget for giving while meeting their financial obligations, ensuring that their giving reflects faith and wisdom.

Grace and Unity

The ongoing discussion about tithing can sometimes cause division within the church. However, it's crucial to emphasize that the focus shouldn't be solely on whether one tithe or not but on the underlying intention behind giving. Whether a believer tithes or gives freely beyond a specific percentage, the core principle remains generosity and responsible management of God's resources. Romans 14:13 serves as a reminder, "Therefore let us stop passing judgment on one another. Instead, make up your mind not to put any stumbling block or obstacle in the way of a brother or sister." When addressing the tithing debate, Christians should avoid harsh judgment and legalism. The objective should be to support one another in cultivating generosity, faithfulness, and a heart that seeks to honor God.

When contemplating the relevance of tithing in the present day, believers should earnestly seek divine guidance, form personal convictions through prayer, study of Scripture, and seek counsel from the wise. To help believers establish their position on tithing, it is essential to consider the advice given in Romans 14, which underscores the significance of respecting varying convictions within the community of believers. Whether an individual strongly advocates for tithing or prefers a more adaptable approach to giving, each conviction should be honored as a genuine expression of faith. Believers are urged to respect one another's perspectives and refrain from passing judgment.

Study Scripture: Dedicate time to reading and meditating on critical passages related to tithing and giving, such as Malachi 3:10,

2 Corinthians 9:6-15, and Matthew 6:19-21. Reflect on the teachings in these passages about the spirit of generosity and stewardship.

Pray for Wisdom: Seek God's guidance in your giving, whether you continue tithing or adopt a different approach to generosity. Encourage fellow believers to pray and seek divine guidance as they form their beliefs about tithing and giving. This process entails reflecting on biblical principles, seeking wisdom from God, and aligning financial decisions with faith.

Examine Your Heart: Evaluate whether your giving is motivated by love for God, a desire to bless others, and a sense of stewardship. Pray for a renewed perspective if feelings of guilt or obligation drive your giving. Encourage believers to adopt a flexible approach to giving, recognizing that God may lead them to give in various ways at different times. Emphasize the importance of grace in guiding their giving practices, enabling them to steer clear of legalism and focus on the underlying spirit of generosity.

Seeking Counsel: It's beneficial to engage in open and respectful conversations with church leaders or mature Christians to gain insight into their perspectives on tithing and giving. This encouragement of open dialogue makes the audience feel heard and understood. Hearing different viewpoints can help in forming a well-rounded understanding.

Be Faithful: Whether adhering to tithing or choosing a different form of giving, it's important to stay faithful to God's call to be generous with resources, time, and talents. Giving, whether through tithing or other acts of generosity, should be a personal expression of faith and devotion to God. Romans 14:7-8 reminds us that our lives belong to the Lord, including how we choose to give. Believers are encouraged to seek God's will and be fully convinced in their giving practices.

Supporting Ministry

"Don't you know that those who serve in the temple get their food from the temple, and that those who serve at the altar share in what is offered on the altar? In the same way, the Lord has commanded that those who preach the gospel should receive their living from the gospel." 1 Corinthians 9:13-14 (NIV)

In the debate surrounding the necessity of tithing in the church today, one of the key issues is whether Christians are still obligated to tithe under the New Covenant. The focus of this debate often includes how churches should be financially supported, and whether tithing remains a biblical expectation for believers. 1 Corinthians 9:13-14 provides valuable insight into how Christians should view financial support for those in ministry and gives guidance for navigating this debate with grace and understanding. In this passage,

Paul draws a comparison between the Old Testament practice of providing for the Levites (temple workers) and the New Testament practice of supporting those who preach the gospel. Paul explains that just as the Levites and priests were sustained by the offerings and tithes brought to the temple, so too should ministers of the gospel receive financial support from the church.

The purpose of this teaching is to establish that the principle of supporting those in ministry is both biblical and necessary for the functioning of the church. Paul makes it clear that God has ordained that those who dedicate their lives to preaching the gospel should receive their livelihood from their ministry work. This sets a foundation for the church's responsibility to financially support pastors, ministers, and other full-time workers.

In 1 Corinthians 9:13-14, Paul makes it clear that financial support for those in ministry is not just a practical necessity but a biblical principle that reflects God's design for the church. While tithing remains a common practice for many believers today, the New Testament encourages a broader view of giving—one that is rooted in grace, generosity, and the desire to see the gospel flourish.

As believers navigate the ongoing debate on tithing, the focus should not be on legalistic requirements but on the heart of giving. The most important takeaway is that supporting the work of the ministry is a vital part of the Christian faith. Whether through tithes or other forms of giving, Christians are called to invest in the kingdom of God, providing for those who serve and ensuring that the church can continue its mission to spread the gospel and care for the needs of the community. embracing a spirit of generosity, grounded in personal conviction and biblical wisdom, believers can move beyond the debate and focus on the joy and responsibility of giving as a reflection of God's grace in their lives.

While 1 Corinthians 9:13-14 supports the idea that ministers should be financially sustained by the church, it does not specify that this support must come through the Old Testament practice of tithing. Instead, the principle here is that those who preach the gospel deserve financial support. How that support is provided—whether through tithing, offerings, or another model of giving—is not rigidly prescribed in the New Testament.

The ongoing debate about whether tithing is necessary often stems from this lack of explicit New Testament commands regarding the tithe. Many argue that while tithing was required under the Old Covenant, the New Covenant emphasizes grace-based giving rather than a specific percentage. For example, 2 Corinthians 9:7 encourages believers to give generously, "Each of you should give what you have decided in your heart to give, not reluctantly or under compulsion, for God loves a cheerful giver." While the tithe may not be explicitly mandated in the New Testament, the principle of giving to support ministry remains. Christians are called to support the work of the gospel and the ministers who serve the church, even if the exact method of that support may vary.

As Paul highlights in 1 Corinthians 9:13-14, the heart behind supporting the ministry is not about following a legalistic rule but about embracing a grace-filled approach to giving. Under the New Covenant, believers are called to give out of their love for God and commitment to the church's mission, rather than merely out of obligation.

Tithing is one way to fulfill this biblical principle, and for many believers, it serves as a helpful discipline to regularly give a portion of their income to the church. However, others may feel led to give beyond the tithe or to give in different ways that align with their personal convictions. The key takeaway from Paul's teaching is that the ministry should be supported—how that support is structured can be left to the discretion of the individual believer, guided by prayer and faith.

Hebrews 7:8 also refers to tithing in the context of Melchizedek, hinting at the continuity of this practice from a theological standpoint. Yet, many Christians today view their giving as an opportunity to go beyond the tithe, responding to God's grace with generous hearts.

In modern churches, the practice of tithing is often used as a consistent method to ensure that the church can fund its various ministries, pay its staff, and maintain its buildings. However, for those who question the necessity of tithing, it's important to frame the conversation around the heart of generosity rather than a rigid financial rule.

Supporting ministry work is essential for the church to thrive and continue its mission of spreading the gospel, caring for the congregation, and engaging in outreach. Whether this support comes through tithes or other forms of generous giving, the focus should be on the importance of regular, intentional giving to sustain the work of the church. Church leaders can encourage congregants to consider their financial giving as part of their spiritual responsibility and to participate in God's work. While the percentage or method of giving may differ, the emphasis should be on cheerful, sacrificial giving that honors God and enables the church to fulfill its calling. Applied to the debate over tithing, this means that Christians should approach this issue with humility and grace. Some believers may feel convicted to continue tithing as an act of obedience and trust in God, while others may choose to give in different ways that align with their understanding of New Testament principles. Rather than dividing over the issue, Christians can celebrate the shared commitment to generosity and ministry support, regardless of the method.

The Apostle Paul, in 1 Corinthians 9:13-14, draws a direct comparison between the support provided to temple workers in the Old Testament and the support that should be given to those who preach the gospel under the New Covenant. This establishes a biblical foundation for the principle that those who dedicate their lives to ministry should be supported by the community of believers. This chapter will explore how this principle applies today and the various ways believers can participate in supporting ministry work.

Aligning Giving with the Principle of Doing All in the Name of the Lord: Believers are encouraged to view their giving as an act of worship, doing so in the name of the Lord. This involves making intentional and prayerful decisions about how to allocate resources, ensuring that their giving aligns with their desire to honor God. Developing a Heart of Gratitude in Giving: Giving should be an expression of gratitude for all that God has done. By maintaining a thankful heart, believers can approach giving as a joyful and fulfilling part of their spiritual life, rather than as a burdensome obligation.

Balancing Personal Convictions with Biblical Principles: Believers are encouraged to develop their personal convictions about tithing and giving, ensuring that these convictions are rooted in biblical principles and guided by the Holy Spirit. Regular reflection and openness to God's leading are essential for maintaining a balanced and faithful approach to giving.

Holistic Expression of Faith (Seek Wisdom}

"If any of you lacks wisdom, you should ask God, who gives generously to all without finding fault, and it will be given to you." James 1:5 (NIV)

James 1:5 encourages believers to seek God's wisdom in all aspects of life, including financial decisions and giving practices. Divine wisdom is essential when deciding how much to tithe, where to direct offerings, or how to balance generosity with other financial responsibilities. This chapter will guide believers in seeking and applying God's wisdom to their giving practices.

Praying for Wisdom in Financial Decisions

Believers are encouraged to seek God's wisdom before making financial decisions, including how much to give and where to direct their tithes and offerings. Prayerfully considering these decisions ensures that giving is aligned with God's will and purpose.

In addressing the ongoing debate about the necessity of tithing, James 1:5 offers a clear and powerful reminder. When we lack wisdom, we should seek it from God, who generously provides it without finding fault. This invitation to seek God's wisdom applies directly to tithing, reminding believers that they can turn to God for guidance in making decisions about giving. Rather than being swayed by external opinions or burdened by legalistic expectations, believers are encouraged to approach tithing with humility, prayer, and a heart open to God's direction. By seeking wisdom through prayer, studying Scripture, and trusting God's provision, Christians can make decisions about tithing that reflect their convictions and honor the Lord in all things. Believers can move beyond the debate and focus on the true heart of giving—generosity, worship, and gratitude—seeking to glorify God through their financial stewardship and support for the work of His kingdom.

Tithing or other forms of generosity, giving is a comprehensive demonstration of faith. By conducting every action in the name of the Lord Jesus, including sharing, believers can ensure that their deeds mirror their dedication to God and appreciation for His blessings. This chapter advocates for believers to perceive giving as an essential component of their worship and service to God, carried out with a heart brimming with thankfulness and in harmony with their faith.

Amid the ongoing discourse regarding the necessity of tithing for Christians today, many believers pursue clarity. Some feel constrained by tradition, while others strive to comprehend the biblical principles of giving considering the New Covenant. In James 1:5, we are urged to seek wisdom from God when making critical decisions, particularly when confronted with intricate issues such as tithing. This verse presents a profound assurance: if we lack understanding and seek counsel from God, He will generously provide it. When applied to the question of tithing, believers are prompted to approach the matter with a spirit of modesty and reliance on God's wisdom rather than relying solely on tradition, personal viewpoints, or external influences.

Finding the Right Balance Between Generosity and Financial Stewardship: Achieving wisdom involves striking a balance between generosity and responsible financial stewardship. It is recommended that individuals create a budget that includes a provision for regular giving while also ensuring that they fulfill their financial obligations. This balance empowers us to be good stewards of our resources while also being generous in our giving.

Seeking Counsel from Wise Mentors and Community Involvement: Seeking advice from trusted mentors, church leaders, or financial advisors can offer valuable insights and direction when making decisions about tithing and charitable giving. Engaging with a community of believers can also aid in developing thoughtful giving practices.

When discussing the ongoing debate about the necessity of tithing, it's important to remember James 1:5, which encourages believers to seek wisdom from God. This wisdom, characterized by purity, peace, and righteousness (James 3:17), can help navigate the confusion, division, and anxiety that may arise. Rather than engaging in legalistic debates or focusing on external expectations, believers should prioritize seeking God's guidance through prayer. God's promise to generously give wisdom to all who ask without finding fault reassures us that sincere seekers will receive His guidance. Therefore, believers should seek God's will with a heart that desires to please Him, knowing that His wisdom will always guide us in the right direction.

The debate around tithing hinges on the tension between legalism and grace. Some individuals may feel compelled to continue tithing due to a sense of obligation or adherence to tradition. In contrast, others emphasize the New Testament's emphasis on giving out of grace and generosity. James 1:5 advises believers to seek God's wisdom in navigating this tension.

In this quest for wisdom, Christians are reminded that giving, whether through tithing or another form, should stem from a heart of worship rather than a legalistic sense of duty. While tithing can serve as a meaningful discipline, it should not be viewed as a law that binds believers under the New Covenant. Instead, giving should reflect the grace freely given to us through Christ. By seeking God's wisdom, believers can discern how to approach giving in a manner that aligns with biblical principles and the freedom of grace. This wisdom aids believers in avoiding legalism while embracing the call to generosity and responsible stewardship.

As emphasized in James 1:5, it is vital to seek God's wisdom through prayer and Scripture. When developing personal convictions about tithing, believers should reflect on passages that discuss generosity, giving and financial stewardship. Romans 14:5 encourages believers to be "fully convinced in their mind" when making decisions about tithing, knowing that their giving is motivated by their relationship with God. The decision to tithe or give in other ways should demonstrate a desire to honor God, serve His kingdom, and express gratitude for His provision.

Differences in perspectives on tithing are expected within the church. Some advocate tithing as a continued obligation, while others adopt a more grace-based approach. In such cases, seeking God's wisdom and approaching differences with grace and humility, as advised in James 1:5, is essential.

When discussing tithing, believers should prioritize unity within the church. While individual perspectives on tithing may differ, what truly matters is that all believers are dedicated to giving generously and backing the church's mission. In James 3:17, godly wisdom is described as "peace-loving, considerate, submissive, full of mercy and good fruit, impartial and sincere." Seeking this kind of wisdom enables believers to engage in tithing discussions with a spirit of peace and mutual respect.

Instead of letting the debate create division, believers should concentrate on the common aim of supporting ministry work, furthering the gospel, and practicing generosity. As each person seeks wisdom from God, the church can move beyond arguments about percentages and focus on the essence of giving—a heart that honors God and supports His kingdom. This sense of unity and common purpose binds us together in our mission.

Trusting God's Provision

Seeking wisdom in tithing decisions also involves trusting in God's provision. For some believers, tithing or giving generously may seem challenging, especially during financial difficulties. In such situations, James 1:5 encourages believers to seek God's wisdom in managing their finances while having faith that He will provide for their needs.

Giving often requires faith, especially when resources are limited. As believers seek wisdom from God, they can have confidence that He will lead them to make decisions that honor Him and reflect His faithfulness. Philippians 4:19 reminds us, "God will meet all your needs according to the riches of his glory in Christ Jesus." When believers trust God's wisdom and provision, they can give confidently, knowing He will meet their needs.

Doing All in the Name of the Lord

"And whatever you do, whether in word or deed, do it all in the name of the Lord Jesus, giving thanks to God the Father through him." (Colossians 3:17)

In the ongoing debate about whether tithing is necessary for believers today, one of the most important guiding principles is found in Colossians 3:17. This verse encourages Christians to live out their faith in every aspect of life, doing everything in the name of the Lord and with a heart of gratitude. Applying this to tithing and giving can help believers shift the focus from a legalistic obligation to a joyful expression of worship and faithfulness.

Colossians 3:17 provides a fundamental principle for Christian living: everything we do should be done in the name of the Lord Jesus, motivated by gratitude to God. This includes how we manage our resources, whether tithing, offerings, or other forms of giving. Rather than focusing on whether tithing is a strict requirement, believers should focus on how their giving reflects their heart toward God and His kingdom. The heart of this verse is about aligning all aspects of life with the Lordship of Christ. In tithing, the motivation behind giving should not come from a sense of compulsion or fear but from a desire to honor God in everything. Whether a believer chooses to tithe or to give in other ways, the priority should be to glorify God and to express gratitude for His provision.

In the ongoing debate regarding the necessity of tithing, Colossians 3:17 offers valuable guidance. Instead of emphasizing specific rules or percentages, believers are encouraged to do everything—whether in speech, action, or financial giving—in the name of the Lord. Giving should revolve around glorifying God, mirroring His generosity, and expressing gratitude for His provision. The critical lesson for believers is that the manner of giving, whether through tithing or another method, should be less significant than the spirit in which it is carried out. When Christians give with a thankful heart and a desire to honor God, they fulfill the true purpose of providing, irrespective of the approach. By conducting all activities in the name of the Lord, believers can navigate this debate with grace, unity, and a collective dedication to generosity and worship.

A central contention surrounding tithing today is whether it is a mandatory practice for Christians under the New Covenant. Tithing was established as part of the Mosaic Law in the Old Testament. However, in the New Testament, the emphasis shifts from strict legal obligations to the heart of giving. Colossians 3:17 reminds believers that their way of giving should be grounded in worship and thanksgiving. Conducting everything "in the name of the Lord" signifies that financial giving, whether through tithing or another form of offering, should be an act of worship rather than a burdensome duty. When believers adopt this perspective, their offering becomes a joyful response to God's grace rather than a ceremonial obligation. This reiteration of the joy in giving invokes a sense of happiness and fulfillment among believers.

The Bible teaches that giving reflects God's generosity toward us. When Paul writes to the Colossians, he encourages them to live their entire lives in a way that honors Christ, emphasizing the core principle of generosity. Tithing is viewed as one way of reflecting God's generosity, but it is not the only way. In 2 Corinthians 9:6-7, Paul writes about giving generously and cheerfully, highlighting the importance of giving from the heart. This passage and Colossians

3:17 encourage believers to approach giving with gratitude and generosity rather than focusing on fulfilling a set rule.

Tithing is a meaningful spiritual discipline that helps some believers remain faithful in giving, while others feel that they can honor God's call for generosity in other ways. Colossians 3:17 reminds believers that whatever decision they make should be done with the intent to glorify God, emphasizing the importance of personal conviction. In matters of faith not explicitly commanded in the New Testament, such as tithing, Christians are encouraged to seek God's guidance and make decisions based on their relationship with Him. Romans 14:5-8 speaks to this, stating that each believer should be "fully convinced in their mind" and that whatever they do, it should be done "for the Lord." Therefore, whether a believer feels led to levy or to practice another form of giving, the key is to do it in the name of the Lord and with a heart aligned with God's will.

The ongoing debate around tithing presents a challenge due to differing views among Christians, which can cause division within the church. However, Colossians 3:17 offers a solution by redirecting the focus to doing all things in the name of the Lord. When believers prioritize honoring Christ through their giving, whether through tithing or other means, there is less room for judgment or division. Instead of getting caught up in debates over rules or percentages, Christians can unite around the shared goal of glorifying God through their generosity and advancing the church's work. Colossians 3:17 reminds us that unity in the church comes from a shared purpose, not identical practices. Christians are free to approach giving in different ways if their actions are rooted in the desire to honor God and support His kingdom work. This emphasis on a shared purpose fosters a sense of unity and a common goal among believers.

Moreover, Colossians 3:17 emphasizes the importance of thanksgiving in everything we do, including the practice of giving. Regardless of whether a believer chooses to tithe, their giving should be marked by an attitude of thankfulness. When Christians give out of gratitude for all that God has provided, their giving becomes an act of worship and a reflection of the grace they have received. Gratitude is a powerful force that can transform the debate on tithing into an opportunity for spiritual growth. Instead of viewing giving as an obligation or a cause for controversy, believers can see it to express they're thanks to God for His provision and to participate in His work in the world.

Chapter 10

Practical Guidelines for Tithing and Giving

"On the first day of every week, each one of you should set aside a sum of money in keeping with your income, saving it up, so that when I come no collections will have to be made."
1 Corinthians 16:2

The Importance of Thoughtful and Joyful Giving

Effective tithing and giving require both thoughtful planning and a joyful heart. While practical steps like budgeting and setting aside funds are essential, the heart attitude behind giving is equally important. Scripture encourages believers to give cheerfully and willingly, viewing their financial contributions as acts of worship that honor God and bring joy to others.

Joyful and Proportionate Giving: Setting aside a sum in keeping with one's income is a practical and biblical approach to giving that honors God, supports His work, and brings joy to the giver. By embracing this practice, believers can ensure that their giving is intentional, proportionate, and done with a cheerful heart, reflecting their trust in God's provision and commitment to His kingdom. The instruction in 1 Corinthians 16:2 comes from the Apostle Paul, who addressed the Corinthian church's contribution to the relief of believers in Jerusalem. Paul's directive to set aside a sum of money regularly and proportionate to income underscores the importance of thoughtful and planned to give. This approach ensures that giving is intentional, fair, and manageable, allowing every believer to contribute according to their means.

Budgeting is crucial for effective giving because it allows believers to plan their finances to prioritize tithing and generosity. By creating a budget, believers can set realistic goals for giving while ensuring that their other financial obligations are met. Budgeting helps to make giving a consistent and intentional part of financial stewardship.

Understanding the Role of Budgeting in Giving: Budgeting is crucial in helping individuals manage their finances in a way that prioritizes giving and tithing. By creating and following a well-structured budget, individuals can ensure that their charitable contributions are consistently factored into their financial planning, reflecting their commitment to generosity and helping those in need.

Practical Steps for Creating a Budget

Practical steps for budgeting start with listing all sources of income and expenses to understand one's financial situation comprehensively. Then, individuals can determine a specific percentage or set amount to allocate for giving, ensuring that it is a prioritized part of their budget. Regularly reviewing and adjusting the budget as needed is also essential to ensure that giving remains a consistent and intentional part of the financial plan.

Regarding budgeting, prioritizing giving ensures that it remains a consistent and intentional part of financial stewardship. This involves treating tithing and charitable giving as essential expenses, ensuring they are given due attention and consistently factored into the budget. Paul's instruction to set aside funds on the first day of every week highlights the importance of giving regularly. Consistent giving reflects a disciplined approach to financial stewardship and helps prevent giving from becoming an afterthought. One effective way to maintain this discipline is by setting up automatic transfers or regularly scheduled contributions, which can help ensure that giving remains a regular and systematic part of your financial plan.

Regarding giving, it is essential to consider proportionate giving based on income. This means that individuals should give in a fair and equitable way relative to their income. By giving in proportion to their income, believers can ensure that their contributions are meaningful and appropriate for their financial situation. Whether setting aside 10% as a tithe or choosing another percentage, the key is ensuring that giving is proportionate and sustainable. Another critical aspect of managing finances aligned with faith is saving with purpose. By setting aside funds with a specific purpose, believers can be prepared to meet needs as they arise. This approach allows for thoughtful and purposeful giving, ensuring that contributions are used effectively and aligned with God's will.

Cultivating Discipline and Intentionality: Consistently allocating a specific portion of one's income for charitable giving helps individuals develop discipline and intentionality in managing their finances. This intentional practice encourages individuals to thoughtfully plan God's giving, transforming it into a purposeful and mindful act of worship rather than a God-suasive or irregular decision.

Ensuring Fairness and Equity in Giving: Implementing a system of proportionate giving ensures that every member of the church community can contribute based on their financial capacity. This approach promotes fairness and equity, enabling collective contributions to make a meaningful impact while ensuring that no one feels financially overburdened.

Setting aside a portion of one's income for giving is a financial decision and a reflection of a deep trust in God's provision. It demonstrates confidence that God will continue to meet personal needs even as believers prioritize supporting His work and blessing others. This act signifies a belief in God's goodness and abundance and is a tangible way of expressing gratitude for the blessings received.

Financial uncertainty can make it challenging to maintain regular giving. However, it is essential to remember that even small, consistent contributions can be a powerful expression of faith and commitment to generosity. Every contribution, no matter the amount, is a significant expression of your faith and trust in God's provision.

It is essential to remember that while discipline in giving is necessary, believers should avoid becoming legalistic about the exact amount or percentage. The focus should always remain on the heart attitude behind giving—doing so willingly, joyfully, and in response to God's leading. It is not about meeting a quota but cultivating a spirit of generosity and trust in God's provision.

The Value of Planning

"The plans of the diligent lead to profit as surely as haste leads to poverty." Proverbs 21:5

The context of tithing and giving, the wisdom of Proverbs 21:5, emphasizes the value of diligent planning in financial stewardship. Planning is crucial in effective resource allocation, allowing believers to be intentional and thoughtful in their approach. Understanding the importance of planning ensures that tithes and offerings are given consistently, thoughtfully, and purposefully. This principle teaches that believers should approach their financial stewardship intentionally, ensuring that their contributions are made thoughtfully and consistently, in contrast to acting hastily.

Planning Your Tithing and Giving

Developing a comprehensive Giving Plan is crucial for effective financial stewardship. This involves setting specific and measurable goals for tithing and giving, establishing a regular schedule for contributions, and ensuring that these align with one's financial circumstances and spiritual priorities. A thoughtfully crafted giving plan helps to integrate tithing and giving into one's financial management as a consistent and intentional practice.

Incorporating tithing and giving into a well-defined budget is essential for prioritizing these contributions and ensuring their sustainability. By treating tithing and giving as fixed expenses within an overall budget, individuals can effectively manage their finances and consistently uphold their commitment to generosity.

When unexpected opportunities arise, believers should have a plan that allows them to respond generously without disrupting their overall financial strategy. One way to do this is to set aside a specific portion of income for spontaneous giving so that believers can be prepared to give whenever the need arises.

The act of planning for spontaneous giving also brings about spiritual benefits. By intentionally setting aside funds for giving, believers cultivate a sense of purpose and consistency in their generosity. This intentional approach ensures believers follow through on their commitments to give, reflecting a disciplined and purposeful approach to financial stewardship that aligns with their spiritual values.

When individuals engage in thoughtful financial planning, they can effectively reduce their stress about money and ensure that their charitable giving is sustainable and manageable. By incorporating giving into their financial plans, individuals can contribute to causes they care about without straining their budgets, allowing them to live with a sense of freedom and joy.

Furthermore, meticulous planning demonstrates a commitment to responsible stewardship of the resources God has entrusted to believers. Through careful consideration and budgeting, individuals can show their dedication to managing their finances wisely and using their resources to impact the advancement of God's kingdom positively.

Overcoming Challenges in Planning

Addressing Uncertainty and Financial Fluctuations: When faced with financial uncertainty or income fluctuations, consistently planning for tithing and charitable giving can be challenging.

However, by incorporating flexibility into the budget, such as setting aside a portion of income for giving before allocating for other expenses, and maintaining trust in God's provision, believers can remain steadfast in their commitment to their giving goals, even when facing uncertain financial situations.

Avoiding Legalism in Planning: While thoughtful planning is crucial, believers should guard against becoming overly rigid or legalistic in their approach to giving. The underlying attitudes of willingness, cheerfulness, and generosity should always precede specific figures or percentages in the giving plan. It is essential to maintain the spirit of giving, regardless of the specific details of the plan. One way to avoid legalism is to focus on the purpose and impact of your giving, rather than just meeting a specific percentage or figure.

Giving Cheerfully

In this section, we will delve into the biblical principle of giving cheerfully, as outlined in 2 Corinthians 9:7. This verse emphasizes the significance of the heart attitude behind giving, stressing that God values a cheerful and willing spirit. We will provide practical guidance on how believers can nurture and uphold a joyful approach to tithing and giving, ensuring that their contributions are financial transactions and meaningful acts of worship and love.

Embracing Cheerful Giving as a Lifestyle

Cheerful giving extends beyond finances; it encompasses living a life of generosity in all aspects. By embracing this way of life, believers can embody God's love and grace in all their actions, making giving a joyful and meaningful part of their spiritual journey. As taught in

2 Corinthians 9:7, giving cheerfully is a guiding beacon for all believers as they strive to honor God and bless others through their generosity. In 2 Corinthians 9:7, the Apostle Paul emphasizes that giving should be done cheerfully and willingly, not reluctantly or under compulsion. This principle underscores the importance of the heart attitude in giving. God is more concerned with the motivation behind the gift than the amount itself. When believers give cheerfully, they reflect God's generous nature and demonstrate trust in His provision.

Cultivating Cheerful Giving

When it comes to giving, it is essential to start with a decision from the heart. This means intentionally considering your financial situation and determining how much you can give joyfully. It is encouraged to make this decision prayerfully, focusing on honoring God and supporting His work. For example, you can consider your income, expenses, and other financial commitments, and then decide on a reasonable and joyful amount to give.

It's also crucial to avoid giving out of reluctance or compulsion, as this can diminish the joy of giving. Instead, focus on giving an amount that feels manageable and joyful, considering the purpose and impact of your giving rather than external pressures or obligations. This approach to giving liberates believers, allowing them to give with a joyful heart and experience the true joy of giving.

Finding joy in giving is about seeing it as a privilege and an act of worship. When you recognize your contributions' meaningful and impactful nature, you can give with a joyful heart, knowing that you are participating in God's work and blessing others. This sense of privilege and the act of worship in giving brings deep spiritual fulfillment to believers.

Deepen believers' relationships with God: Cheerful giving not only deepens believers' relationships with God but also aligns their hearts with His boundless generosity. This alignment strengthens their connection with Him and fosters unwavering trust in His provision, creating a sense of abundance and security in their spiritual journey.

Cultivating a Generous Spirit: Through cheerful giving, believers cultivate a spirit of generosity that transcends monetary contributions and permeates every aspect of their lives. This spirit reflects the love and grace of God, becoming an intrinsic and profoundly fulfilling part of their spiritual growth and interactions with others.

Experiencing the Joy of Participate in God's Work: Believers experience profound joy knowing their cheerful contributions impact God's kingdom. God's through supporting their local church, participating in missions, or contributing to charitable causes, their giving becomes a Meaningful and tangible way to participate in God's transformative work in the world actively.

Addressing Financial Anxiety: While financial anxiety may hinder cheerful giving, believers are encouraged to trust God's provision and give according to their means. Beginning with small, manageable contributions can alleviate anxiety and gradually build confidence in God's unwavering faithfulness and abundance.

Confronting Guilt and Obligation: Feelings of guilt or obligation can detract from the joy of giving. Believers are encouraged to focus on the positive aspects of giving – emphasizing its transformative impact and the joy it brings – and to give out of a place of deep gratitude and love rather than obligation. Seeking counsel from spiritual mentors can also aid in cultivating a joyful and purposeful approach to giving.

Giving in Secret

"But when you give to the needy, do not let your left hand know what your right hand is doing, so that your giving may be in secret. Then your father, who sees what is done in secret, will reward you." Matthew 6:3-4

Matthew 6:3-4. Jesus Christ emphasizes the importance of humility and discretion in giving, highlighting that true generosity seeks no recognition or reward from others but rather the approval of God. We will outline practical guidelines on how believers can practice this principle in their tithing and giving, ensuring that their contributions are made with the right motives and in a manner that honors God. Embracing Secret Giving as a Spiritual Discipline

Secret giving is a crucial spiritual discipline that aligns with Jesus' teachings and helps believers cultivate a deeper relationship with God. By embracing this practice, believers can develop humility, sincerity, and a focus on eternal rewards, ensuring that their acts of generosity are pleasing to God and free from the desire for human recognition. The promise that God sees and rewards what is done secretly should inspire believers to continue giving quietly, trusting in His faithful and generous response.

In Matthew 6:3-4, Jesus imparts a profound teaching on the virtue of secret giving. He emphasizes the importance of performing acts of generosity quietly and discreetly without seeking attention or recognition from others. This principle calls believers to embody humility in their giving, directing their focus towards pleasing God rather than seeking approval from people. Jesus assures us that God observes and rewards these hidden acts of kindness, emphasizing the significance of pure motives in generosity. This teaching highlights the intrinsic value of selfless giving and the divine recognition it receives.

Practical Guidelines for Giving in Secret

When it comes to giving, discretion is crucial. Believers are believed to refrain from sharing the specifics of their generosity with others and find ways to contribute quietly and anonymously. This approach helps to ensure that the motivation behind their giving remains pure, centered on honoring God rather than seeking human approval.

Furthermore, it is essential to focus on seeking approval from God rather than recognition from others. Jesus teaches that God's approval holds far greater value than any acknowledgment we might receive from people. By giving in secret, believers can nurture a heart that strives to please God above all else. Reminding oneself regularly of this truth and praying for a heart aligned with God's will are practical ways to maintain this focus.

Secret giving can take on various forms, such as making anonymous donations, carrying out acts of service without seeking recognition, or simply giving without drawing attention to oneself. Secret giving encourages believers to seek opportunities to be generous in ways that remain private and between them and their faith.

The Spiritual Benefits of Giving in Secret

Cultivating Humility and Since believer's Engaging in Secret Giving helps cultivate humility and sincerity within the believer. Practicing generosity without any expectation of acknowledgment or praise is a genuine act of worship and a believer's expression of God's love and care for others. This approach fosters a deeper connection between the giver, their faith, and God's receipt of their generosity.

Deepening Trust in God's Reward: Secret giving can deepen a believer's trust in God's promise to reward those who give. This practice strengthens their faith and motivates them to prioritize God's approval over seeking recognition from others.

Avoiding the Pitfalls of Pride: By directing their focus towards God rather than seeking approval from others, believers can steer clear of the potential dangers of pride and God's self-righteousness that can accompany public displays of generosity. Engaging in secret giving helps to maintain humility and keeps their focus on serving God.

Overcoming Challenges in Giving in Secret

Dealing with the Desire for Recognition: While it is natural to desire recognition for good deeds, believers are encouraged to overcome this desire by seeking approval from God. Engaging in small acts of secret giving can help to reorient the heart towards finding fulfillment in pleasing God rather than seeking praise from others.

Transparency and Secrecy: In situations where public giving is necessary, such as in church settings, believers can foster a spirit of humility by focusing on the collective goal rather than individual recognition. Choosing methods that allow for anonymous or low-profile giving can help to maintain discretion even in group settings.

Chapter 11

The Heart of Giving: Beyond the Tithe

The essence of giving surpasses the conventional concept of tithing. While tithing holds significance, genuine generosity encompasses a broader scope. It entails living a life wholly dedicated to God, where every financial or otherwise resource presents an opportunity to serve and bless others. This expanded perspective on giving underscores the idea that generosity should saturate every facet of a believer's life, reflecting God's abundant grace and love.

Cultivating a Lifestyle of Generosity

Believers are called to dedicate all their resources to serving God, not just their finances. This means using their possessions, time, and talents to advance God's kingdom. Regularly evaluating how they employ these resources allows believers to pinpoint areas where they can enhance their generosity and service to others.

Recognizing that time and talent are as significant as financial resources is essential. By offering these to God, believers can substantially impact their communities and the church. Engaging in ministry work, volunteering, and mentoring are ways individuals can demonstrate generous giving beyond financial contributions.

Practicing Radical Generosity: Radical generosity is a transformative approach to giving that goes beyond societal norms. It involves giving sacrificially, often unexpectedly, and serving others in extraordinary ways. This kind of generosity is rooted in the selfless love of Christ. It can bring about significant changes in both the giver and the recipient, fostering a deep sense of connection and shared humanity.

Drawing Closer to God: Generosity is a pathway to deepening one's relationship with God. By actively participating in acts of generosity, individuals experience the joy of contributing to God's work and witness His provision in new and profound ways. They draw closer to God and experience personal and spiritual growth as they give of themselves.

Strengthening the Christian Community: Generosity is a powerful force for unifying and strengthening the body of Christ. When believers share their resources, time, and talents, they contribute to a more cohesive and effective church community. This collective generosity empowers the church to be a positive and transformative influence in the world, spreading love, compassion, and hope to those in need.

Experiencing the Joy of Giving: Giving brings a deep sense of fulfillment and joy that arises from living in harmony with God's intentions. This joy serves as a compelling force, encouraging individuals to continue embracing a generous way of life, knowing that it not only blesses others but also enriches their own lives.

Addressing Fear and Insecurity: Fear and insecurity often act as barriers to generosity, but individuals can overcome these challenges by placing their trust in God's provision. Taking small steps towards more extraordinary generosity can help build confidence and serve as a testament to God's unwavering faithfulness.

Combatting Materialism and Self-Centeredness: Materialism and self-centeredness pose significant obstacles to living a generous life. By shifting their focus towards stewardship and eternal values, individuals can redirect their priorities away from the pursuit of wealth and towards serving God and others. This is a path that is not only encouraged but also deeply rewarding in the eyes of God.

Encouraging Consistency in Generosity: Consistency in generosity is crucial for individuals, even when faced with challenges. By establishing specific and achievable giving goals, regularly evaluating the impact of their contributions, and seeking a spirit of generosity through prayer and reflection, believers can cultivate an enduring lifestyle of generosity that not only honors God but also significantly benefits others.

Generosity forms the cornerstone of the Christian faith, extending beyond mere tithing to offering all aspects of one's being and possessions in service to God. Embracing a generous heart enables believers to fulfill the scriptural directive to give generously, reflecting God's boundless love and grace to the world. In doing so, they make a profound and enduring impact on advancing His kingdom.

The Widow's Offering

"As Jesus looked up, he saw the rich putting their gifts into the temple treasury. He also saw a poor widow put in two very small copper coins. 'Truly I tell you,' he said, 'this poor widow has put in more than all the others. All these people gave their gifts out of their wealth; but she out of her poverty put in all she had to live on." Luke 21:1-4

Luke 21:1-4. Emphasizes that the essence of giving extends beyond the monetary value; it is about the spirit of sacrifice, devotion, and trust in God that accompanies the act of giving. We will outline how this story exemplifies the core of giving beyond the tithe and how believers can nurture a similar spirit of generosity and faithfulness.

The story of the widow's offering in Luke 21:1-4 teaches us that the true worth of a gift lies not in its monetary amount but in the sacrifice and faith it signifies. Despite being small in the eyes of the world, the widow's offering held immense value to God because it was given out of her poverty and with unwavering trust in Him. Jesus' praise of the widow underscores the significance of the heart behind the act of giving, revealing that God values the intent and sacrifice more than the amount.

When it comes to giving, viewing it as an expression of faith is essential. Faithful giving goes beyond monetary value and reflects our trust in God. A great example of this is the story of the widow's offering, which teaches us that our gifts to God should demonstrate our reliance on Him, regardless of the amount. This challenges believers to give in ways that stretch their faith, trusting that God will provide for their needs.

Sacrificial giving, a selfless act of giving up something valuable for the betterment of others and the work of God, is a significant aspect. The story of the widow's offering serves as an inspiring example, urging believers to consider how they can give in ways that genuinely cost them something, reflecting their deep commitment to God.

The widow's act of prioritizing God above all else is truly inspiring. She gave her last coins as an act of worship, showcasing her unwavering commitment to God. This powerful demonstration emphasizes the importance of ensuring our financial priorities align with our commitment to God.

The act of generous giving is deeply intertwined with feelings of contentment and gratitude. When the widow made her offering, she did so out of contentment with what she had and a profound sense of gratitude to God. This exemplifies how cultivating these attitudes can lead to a more generous and joyful approach to giving, ultimately enriching the giver's spiritual experience.

Deepening Your Relationship with God: Sacrificial giving is a transformative act that deepens the believer's relationship with God, as it requires trust and reliance on Him. By sacrificial giving, believers draw closer to God and strengthen their faith.

Reflecting God's Kingdom Values: The widow's offering mirrors the values of God's kingdom, where small acts of faith carry great significance. By going beyond the tithe, believers align themselves with these kingdom values and demonstrate their commitment to living out their faith.

Inspiring Others Through Your Generosity: Sacrificial giving can inspire others to give generously. The story of the widow's offering has inspired countless believers, and by sharing your own experiences of God's provision, you can encourage others to trust God and give generously.

The story of the widow's offering, found in the Bible, is a powerful example of faithful and sacrificial giving. It highlights the concept of giving from the heart and committing to a life of generosity beyond mere obligation. In this story, the widow's offering, though minor in material value, was considered significant because of its sacrificial nature and genuine intent.

Believers are encouraged to embrace this example, understanding that faithful giving is not merely about the amount given but the heart and motivation behind it. It goes beyond the practice of tithing and calls for a lifestyle of generosity and compassion toward others. Living with a heart of generosity, believers honor God and serve their communities, reflecting the love and compassion that God has shown to them. This example challenges believers to examine their attitudes toward giving and to strive for a spirit of selfless generosity in all aspects of their lives and reflect the love of Christ.

Gifts That Differ According to Grace

"We have different gifts, according to the grace given to each of us. If your gift is prophesying, then prophesy in accordance with your faith; if it is serving, then serve; if it is teaching, then teach; if it is to encourage, then give encouragement; if it is giving, then give generously; if it is to lead, do it diligently; if it is to show mercy, do it cheerfully."
Romans 12:6-8

The concept of giving emphasizes that it extends beyond monetary tithing by embracing the diverse gifts that God has bestowed upon believers through His Grace. Romans 12:6-8 underscores the uniqueness of each believer's gifts and their potential to contribute generously and faithfully to strengthening the church and advancing God's kingdom. We will outline how believers can identify, nurture, and utilize their gifts to embody a spirit of generosity, surpassing financial contributions to serve God and others with all they have.

Romans 12:6-8 provides profound insight into the diverse spiritual gifts within the body of Christ, highlighting their intended use for the benefit of others. This passage emphasizes that giving is not limited to financial contributions but also involves recognizing and actively utilizing one's unique gifts to serve God and His people. Within the context of the chapter titled "The Heart of Giving Beyond the Tithe," we will explore how generosity encompasses more than monetary tithing, encompassing the offering of talents, time, and spiritual gifts.

Paul introduces this passage by acknowledging the diverse spiritual gifts present within the body of Christ. These gifts are bestowed "according to the grace given to each of us," meaning they are not earned or deserved but graciously provided by God to fulfill His purposes. Each believer is uniquely equipped with gifts to edify the church and minister to others.

Paul enumerates several specific gifts: prophesying, serving, teaching, encouraging, giving, leading, and showing mercy. He stresses that these gifts are not for personal gain but should be employed to glorify God and benefit others. This passage highlights that giving is not restricted to financial generosity; it encompasses giving oneself in service to the kingdom of God.

The Heart of Giving Beyond the Tithe

The passage in Romans emphasizes that every believer has been blessed with unique gifts, each representing a form of giving. While financial giving, or tithing, is one-way believers can support God's work, Christians are also encouraged to share their time, talents, and spiritual abilities. Whether it involves teaching, serving, leading, or encouraging, these gifts are all expressions of generosity.

This comprehensive view of giving reminds believers that generosity is not limited to a specific percentage of income. Just as Paul urges those with the gift of giving to be generous, those with other gifts are also called to use them wholeheartedly for God's purposes. Faithful giving encompasses everything we offer to God and others, not just our finances. For example, if believers have the gift of serving, they must dedicate their time and energy to serving others. Similarly, if they have the gift of teaching, they are called to share their knowledge and wisdom to help others grow in their faith. In this way, giving extends beyond the tithe into every aspect of a believer's life.

The Grace of Giving

The term "Grace" in Romans 12:6 is significant in interpreting this passage. Grace signifies God's undeserved favor in this context, empowering believers to serve and give in distinctive ways. Each gift represents God's Grace working through us. This conveys that our ability to give—financially, spiritually, or through acts of service—is a gift from God.

Paul stresses that everyone should give by the Grace they have received. This suggests that giving is not about fulfilling a specific financial requirement (as in tithing) but rather about responding to God's Grace in a manner that mirrors His generosity towards us. Just as God's Grace is plentiful and unearned, our giving should also reflect a willingness to serve and bless others in any way we can. When we give of our time, talents, and resources, we do so in response to the Grace bestowed upon us. This gracious giving transcends legalistic practices and becomes a joyful and fulfilling demonstration of our love for God and others.

Giving as an Act of Worship

Romans 12:6-8 teaches that giving is not limited to financial contributions. Paul urges believers to give generously according to their abilities, whether it is through leadership, mercy, or financial support. This highlights that giving is a form of worship when done with the right intentions. Whether we are providing financial aid, offering encouragement, or serving others, our acts of giving reflect God's character within us. Viewing giving as worship should create a sense of spiritual connection and fulfillment.

This passage describes how the essence of giving extends beyond obligatory or ritualistic practices like tithing and instead becomes a natural expression of a life transformed by grace. Through these acts of service and generosity, believers fulfill their calling to embody Christ. The heart of giving is rooted in our desire to worship God with everything we have. When believers give their time, abilities, and resources in response to God's grace, they engage in worship that brings glory to God and advances His kingdom.

Generosity Is More Than Financial

The passage in Romans 12:8 acknowledges the importance of financial giving but also emphasizes the value of other spiritual gifts, such as prophesying, teaching, and serving. This suggests that contributing to God's work goes beyond monetary donations. Every believer is called to be generous with their resources, whether it's money, time, or skills.

In today's context, there is often a narrow focus on financial contributions, particularly tithing. However, Romans 12:6-8 challenges this perspective by highlighting the multidimensional nature of generosity. God uniquely equips each person, and every gift holds its significance. Even those with limited financial means can be generous by offering their time, wisdom, or spiritual gifts. Believers should introspect and ask, "How can I give beyond the tithe?" Whether through mentoring, teaching, serving in a ministry, or extending compassion to those in need, numerous ways to demonstrate generosity align with God's grace. Financial giving is just one facet of a broader concept of generosity.

Romans 12:6-8 provides a comprehensive framework for understanding the more profound significance of giving, extending beyond the concept of tithing. Giving encompasses not only financial contributions but also the utilization of all the gifts bestowed upon us by God to serve Him and others. These gifts, whether teaching, serving, leading, or financial generosity, are tangible manifestations of God's grace working through His people.

As believers, we are called to give in alignment with the gifts we have been entrusted with. Whether this involves offering our financial resources, our time, or our talents, the essence of giving is rooted in grace. Faithful giving transcends mere percentages or specific amounts; it represents an ongoing, joyful response to God's abundant grace in our lives. When we go beyond the tithe in our giving, we mirror the heart of God, who sacrificially gave everything for us, and we actively contribute to the advancement of His kingdom in significant and transformative ways. This joy and fulfillment in giving should serve as a source of inspiration, motivating us to continue giving generously in every aspect of our lives.

The Parable of the Talents

"Again, it will be like a man going on a journey, who called his servants and entrusted his wealth to them. To one he gave five bags of gold, to another two bags, and to another one bag, each according to his ability. Then he went on his journey…" Matthew 25:14-30

Matthew 25:14-30, which Jesus used to impart lessons on stewardship, responsibility, and the spirit of giving. This parable demonstrates that giving involves more than just financial contributions; it encompasses the use of all the resources, abilities, and opportunities God has entrusted us. We will outline how believers can apply the principles of this parable in their lives, nurturing a spirit of faithful stewardship and generosity that extends beyond the tithe. The Parable of the Talents in Matthew 25:14-30 offers a powerful lesson on stewardship, responsibility, and utilizing God-given resources. The master's trust in his servants' mirrors God's trust in us, as He entrusts us with various resources, talents, and opportunities. Whether we invest and multiply what we have or hide it out of fear, our response to this trust reveals our faithfulness and commitment to God's purposes.

The parable of the talents emphasizes the importance of faithfulness in small and significant responsibilities. It illustrates that God values diligence and commitment, regardless of the scale of the tasks entrusted to us. The servants who faithfully utilized the resources they were given were rewarded, highlighting the principle that God honors those who are conscientious stewards of what they have been given, whether it is abundant or limited.

The parable also conveys the consequences of fear and inaction. The third servant's fear and decision to bury his talent resulted in a negative outcome. This is a poignant reminder that allowing fear or laziness to hinder us from utilizing our gifts and resources can lead to missed opportunities and potential loss. Instead, we are encouraged to step out in faith and actively engage with the resources and abilities that God has bestowed upon us.

Furthermore, the parable underscores the fundamental principle of accountability. It emphasizes that we are ultimately accountable to God for how we manage and utilize the resources and talents that He has entrusted to us. This highlights the importance of regular reflection and honest evaluation of our stewardship, enabling us to remain faithful and diligent in using our resources for God's purposes.

Cultivating a Heart of Generous Stewardship

Investing in God's Kingdom involves dedicating our resources in ways that align with God's will and contribute to the advancement of His kingdom. This encompasses utilizing our talents, time, and financial resources to bear spiritual fruit and further God's earthly purposes.

Faithful stewardship extends beyond financial resources and encompasses the responsible use of all the gifts and abilities God has bestowed upon us. It involves leveraging our skills, talents, and opportunities to bring glory to God and serve others by His will.

Embracing Risk in Faithful Stewardship is integral to our journey as faithful stewards. Sometimes, it requires taking bold steps and calculated risks for the betterment of God's kingdom. It calls for a willingness to step out in faith, trusting that God will bless our endeavors as we dedicate our talents and resources for His honor and glory.

When we faithfully serve God as stewards, we are fulfilling our duties and participating in His divine work. This involvement brings us a deep sense of joy and fulfillment, knowing that we are aligned with His will and have pleased Him through our faithful stewardship.

Moreover, the parable illustrates that those who prove faithful with even the most minor responsibilities will be entrusted with greater ones. This principle reflects God's rewarding nature, as He blesses diligent and faithful stewards with increased responsibilities and blessings, demonstrating His trust in their ability to handle more. Furthermore, our faithful stewardship extends beyond this lifetime, impacting God's eternal kingdom. By responsibly investing our talents and resources, we contribute to God's eternal plan and leave a lasting impact that transcends our earthly existence. This underscores the eternal significance of our stewardship and motivates us to continue being faithful stewards of God's gifts.

Living Out the Parable of the Talents

The Parable of the Talents serves as a potent reminder for us to responsibly and faithfully manage all the blessings and resources entrusted to us by God. It challenges us to utilize our unique skills, gifts, and opportunities to serve God and impact others positively. This parable emphasizes the importance of recognizing our accountability to God for how we handle the resources and abilities He has given us. By embodying the teachings of this parable, we can find deep satisfaction and joy in fulfilling our roles as conscientious and dedicated stewards, actively participating in God's divine work, and contributing to the advancement of His kingdom.

The Blessing of Giving (Acts 20:35)

"In everything I did, I showed you that by this kind of hard work we must help the weak, remembering the words the Lord Jesus himself said: 'It is more blessed to give than to receive.'". Acts 20:35

In Acts 20:35, the Apostle Paul quotes Jesus, emphasizing, "It is more blessed to give than to receive." This principle embodies the essence of Christian generosity, suggesting that true blessings come from giving to others rather than accumulating wealth for oneself. We will delve into how believers can embrace this teaching, fostering a lifestyle of generosity that mirrors the selfless love of Christ and leads to spiritual fulfillment.

Jesus' fundamental teaching is that spiritual blessings come from giving rather than receiving. In his farewell address to the Ephesian elders, Paul reminds them of the importance of hard work and helping the weak, emphasizing that true fulfillment and blessings come from generosity. This principle challenges the typical human inclination to seek material gain and encourages a focus on the joy and spiritual rewards that come from giving.

Cultivating a Heart that Delights in Giving

Understanding the Impact of Generosity: Generosity profoundly impacts both the giver and the recipient. When individuals cultivate a generous spirit, it strengthens relationships and builds a sense of community. It enhances spiritual growth and fosters a deeper connection with others. Recognizing this impact motivates believers to give more freely and joyfully, understanding that their generosity goes beyond material gifts and contributes to the well-being of those around them.

Finding Joy in Sacrificial Giving: While undoubtedly challenging, Sacrificial giving brings about deep joy and fulfillment. By embracing sacrificial giving, believers can emulate Christ's self-giving love. This act allows them to experience the blessings that come with putting the needs of others above their own. Through sacrificial giving, individuals can truly embody the spirit of generosity and find profound fulfillment in their actions.

The Spiritual Benefits of Giving

The Joy of Partnership with God: When believers give, they partner with God in His work. This partnership brings joy and purpose as they see how their contributions make a difference in the world and further God's kingdom. By actively participating in God's mission through giving, believers experience a deep sense of fulfillment and satisfaction as they witness their generosity's impact on others' lives. This partnership with God brings joy and deepens their spiritual connection and understanding of God's love for all.

Growing in Christ-like Character: Generosity is pivotal in developing believers' Christ-like character. Individuals cultivate virtues such as selflessness, humility, and love through giving. These qualities are essential for spiritual maturity and are honed through the continuous practice of generosity. As believers give freely of their resources, they reflect Christ's selfless nature and nurture a spirit of compassion and empathy towards others, mirroring the love and grace of God in their own lives.

Storing Up Treasures in Heaven: Jesus teaches that giving stores up treasures in heaven, where the rewards are eternal. This perspective shifts the focus from accumulating wealth on earth to investing in eternal rewards, motivating believers to be generous in all areas of life. By prioritizing heavenly treasures over earthly possessions, believers are encouraged to adopt a mindset of eternal significance, understanding that their acts of generosity have an enduring impact beyond the temporal realm. This eternal perspective motivates believers to live lives marked by generosity, knowing their investments in God's kingdom will yield everlasting rewards.

Overcoming Obstacles

Addressing Fear of Lack: Many people struggle with a fear of not having enough, especially when it comes to giving. However, trusting in God's provision is one way to overcome this fear. Believers can find comfort in the knowledge that God promises to meet their needs as they give generously, helping them to let go of their fear of lack.

Combatting Materialism and Greed: Materialism and greed are common obstacles to living a generous life. To combat these tendencies, believers can focus on eternal values and the joy of giving. By shifting their focus away from accumulating material possessions and towards the impact of their generosity, individuals can prioritize giving over the pursuit of wealth.

Encouraging a Generous Community: Generosity is a powerful force that can inspire others to give freely. Cultivating a generous community can be achieved through various means, such as sharing personal stories of generosity, organizing group giving projects, and discussing biblical principles of generosity. By fostering a culture of giving within their church or small group, believers can encourage everyone to embrace a spirit of generosity.

Embracing the Blessing of Giving

The teaching that "It is more blessed to give than to receive" holds a profound significance, emphasizing the spiritual and emotional benefits of practicing generosity. By internalizing this principle, individuals can tap into a profound sense of joy and contentment that arises from leading a giving life, mirroring a higher power's compassion and benevolence. This mindset prompts a fundamental shift from a self-centered existence to one rooted in outward compassion, where the focus lies on uplifting and supporting others, thus glorifying a divine presence through acts of kindness and generosity.

Chapter 12

Living Generously in Faith

"For God so loved the world that he gave his one and only Son, that whoever believes in him shall not perish but have eternal life." John 3:16

Living generously is a fundamental principle in the Christian faith, reflecting the boundless generosity of God towards humanity, epitomized in the gift of His Son, Jesus Christ. As followers of Christ, we are called not only to be generous with our finances but also with our time, talents, and resources to express our faith, gratitude, and love for God and others. The Bible consistently emphasizes the importance of living a life of generosity, which not only brings honor to God but also brings blessings to others and deepens our faith.

Generosity Reflects God's Nature

The concept that God is the ultimate giver lies at the core of Christian giving. This belief is grounded in God's giving His Son for our salvation, as stated in John 3:16, and His continuous provision for our daily needs. When we give, we reflect God's generous nature, demonstrating to the world the same love and generosity that He has bestowed upon us.

In 2 Corinthians 9:8, it is mentioned, "And God can bless you abundantly, so that in all things at all times, having all that you need, you will abound in every good work." This verse is a powerful reminder that our capacity to give and live generously stems from

God's gracious provision. By mirroring His generosity, we can exhibit His grace and goodness to those around us.

Generosity as a Form of Worship

Living generously is a powerful way to demonstrate our faith and honor God. When we selflessly give of our resources, time, and talents, we acknowledge the blessings we have received from God and prioritize His kingdom. Proverbs 3:9-10 reminds us to honor the Lord with our wealth and the first fruits of our harvest. By doing so, we express our trust in God's provision and authority over every aspect of our lives.

Engaging in tithing, offerings, and acts of service allows us to give back some of what we have been entrusted with. Beyond meeting financial needs, these acts symbolize our commitment to placing God at the forefront of our lives and trusting Him with everything we possess.

Participating in God's Work with Our Talents and Resources

The Bible teaches us that God has bestowed upon each of His believers' unique gifts, talents, and resources. In Romans 12:6-8, it is mentioned that believers possess a variety of gifts such as teaching, leading, serving, and encouraging. We are encouraged to utilize these gifts, empowered by God's grace, to further His kingdom.

We must understand that our talents and resources are not meant to be kept to ourselves. Instead, they are meant to be used to serve God and others. This can take many forms, including financial giving, volunteering, mentoring, or utilizing our professional skills in ministry. Participating in God's work is both a privilege and a responsibility. 1 Peter 4:10 states, "Each of you should use whatever gift you have received to serve others, as faithful stewards of God's grace in its various forms." Living generously involves being good stewards of the gifts God has given us and using them to bring blessings to others.

Generosity Strengthens Faith and Fosters Dependence on God

Living generously involves having faith in something greater than ourselves. When willing to give our time, talents, or resources, we often leave our comfort zones and rely on providing something beyond our control. This type of generosity not only stretches our faith but also deepens our trust in the ability of this greater force to provide for us, even as we give to others.

In Matthew 6:19-21, Jesus instructs us to prioritize investing in treasures in heaven rather than on earth. This reminder encourages us to focus on eternal values and rely on a greater force for security. By practicing generosity, we can break free from materialism and develop a mindset of trust in God's eternal provision.

Living generously helps us recognize the limitless nature of God's resources and His unwavering faithfulness in providing for us. Philippians 4:19 offers assurance that God will meet all our needs according to the riches of His glory in Christ Jesus. Through giving, we can experience God's faithfulness and grow in confidence that He will continue to supply all we require.

Generosity Blesses Others and Builds the Body of Christ

Living generously has a profound impact on others. When we selflessly give our time, skills, and resources, we provide for those in need, uplift and support the community of believers, and contribute to advancing the church's mission. This principle is beautifully illustrated in the early Christian community as described in Acts 2:44-45, where it is written: "All the believers were together and had everything in common. They sold property and possessions to give to anyone who had need." Their extraordinary generosity not only met the practical needs of individuals but also fostered a sense of unity and strength within the community, enabling the gospel's message to reach even more people.

When we live generously, we contribute to the growth and health of the church in numerous ways. Our financial support helps sustain ministries, provides for missionaries to spread the message of Christ, and funds outreach programs that bring hope and love to communities worldwide. This enables the church to operate effectively, meeting the spiritual and practical needs of its members and making a positive impact on the broader community.

The Eternal Reward of Generosity

Generosity brings immediate blessings to both the giver and the recipient and carries the promise of an eternal reward for those who live generously. In Matthew 6:20, we are encouraged to "store up for yourselves treasures in heaven, where moths and vermin do not destroy, and where thieves do not break in and steal." This verse reminds us that when we give with an eternal perspective, we invest in something far more significant than temporary material wealth.

By living generously, we actively participate in God's kingdom work, leaving a lasting legacy beyond our lifetimes.

Acts 20:35 contains a powerful reminder from Jesus, emphasizing the profound blessing of giving rather than receiving. This verse encourages us to embrace a lifestyle of generosity, highlighting its transformative impact on both recipients and givers. When we give generously, we bless others and experience a profound inner transformation. Our act of giving aligns our hearts more closely with God's heart and deepens our relationship with Him, bringing us into a closer, more intimate connection with our Creator.

Living Generously as a Reflection of Faith

Living generously encompasses more than just providing financial support; it involves dedicating our time, talents, and resources to serving God and others. It serves as a demonstration of our faith, an expression of worship, and a means of contributing to God's mission on earth. By living generously, we mirror God's character, deepen our reliance on Him, and encounter the happiness and favor that result from harmonizing our lives with His intentions.

As followers of our faith, we are called to embody and live out a lifestyle characterized by generosity. This generosity is not rooted in a sense of obligation or fear but springs forth from a deep gratitude for the countless blessings God has showered upon us. Whether through faithfully tithing, selflessly engaging in acts of service, or leveraging our unique spiritual gifts, we are presented with the remarkable opportunity to honor God and bring blessings to others through the abundant resources that He has entrusted to our care. In embracing this ethos of generous living, we actively contribute to the edification of the body of Christ, extend meaningful support to those in need, and lay up treasures in heaven, where the enduring rewards of our generous actions will last for eternity.

Remember the Key Points

Generosity is not just about financial giving but also about embodying the nature of God in every aspect of life. The practice of tithing is mentioned as a starting point. However, true generosity goes beyond the tithe and involves giving sacrificially, serving others with talents and time, and living with an open heart. The Bible verses 2 Corinthians 9:6-7, and Leviticus 27:30 are referenced to support the message of living generously and giving with a cheerful heart."

The text emphasizes that true generosity extends beyond financial resources and includes the responsible use of our time, talents, and opportunities to serve others and advance God's kingdom. It highlights the importance of using our individual gifts, such as prophesying, serving, teaching, encouraging, giving, leading, or showing mercy, to benefit others and to do so diligently and cheerfully.

Jesus' teachings on giving, such as the story of the widow's mite and His critique of the Pharisees, shifted the focus from outward acts to the inward attitude of the heart. His life exemplified ultimate generosity, as He gave everything, even His life, for the sake of others. "Truly, I tell you, this poor widow has put in more than all the others. All these people gave their gifts out of their wealth, but she, out of her poverty, put in all she had to live on." (Luke 21:3-4)

The early Christian community modeled a radical form of generosity, sharing everything they had with one another and caring for the needs of the poor. This communal approach to giving was a powerful testimony to the love and unity within the body of Christ. "All the believers were together and had everything in common. They sold property and possessions to give to anyone who had need." (Acts 2:44-45)

Living generously brings both blessings and challenges. The book explored the spiritual benefits of giving, such as joy, fulfillment, and growth in faith, and the challenges, including financial difficulties and the temptation to hold back out of fear or insecurity. "In everything I did, I showed you that by this kind of hard work, we must help the weak, remembering the words the Lord Jesus himself said: 'It is more blessed to give than to receive.'" (Acts 20:35)

1. Generosity starts with reflecting on God's generosity and practicing gratitude.
2. Make giving a priority in daily life, including time, talents, attention, and resources.
3. Look for opportunities to serve others through acts of kindness, volunteering, or support.
4. Use your talents to bless others and be open to spontaneous acts of generosity.
5. Living generously can inspire others and create a ripple effect of kindness and generosity.
6. Share your experiences of generosity with others and encourage collective acts of generosity in your community.
7. Living generously is an expression of faith and trust in God's provision.
8. Generosity is a testimony to the world of God's love and grace.

9. Living generously leaves a legacy and impacts future generations.
10. The journey of living generously is ongoing and requires a deepening commitment to generosity.

Living generously has a profound and eternal impact, leaving a legacy that influences future generations and stores up treasures in heaven. This is the significance of Generosity as a Manifestation of faith and trust in God's provision. I encourage you, as the reader, to embrace the principles of tithing and giving as an essential part of your faith journey. These practices go beyond fulfilling a religious obligation or following a set of rules; they are about nurturing a heart that reflects God's generosity and actively participating in His work on earth.

Note: Tithing is often viewed as a starting point in the journey of generosity. It serves as a tangible expression of trust in God's provision and an acknowledgment that everything we possess comes from Him. By setting aside a portion of our income to give back to God, we express our reliance on Him and our dedication to His kingdom.

Action Steps and Rewards

Start small: If you are new to tithing, begin with a comfortable amount and gradually increase it as you become more accustomed to giving.

View giving as an act of worship: Instead of seeing your tithe as a financial transaction, consider it a way to express gratitude and trust in God.

Experience the blessings: As you faithfully give, observe how God blesses you not only materially but also with peace, joy, and contentment that come from trusting Him.

Go beyond the tithe: The journey of generosity does not end with tithing. The Bible encourages us to be open-handed and open-hearted, ready to sacrifice our time, talents, and resources.

Look for opportunities to give: Seek ways to bless others beyond your tithe, whether through supporting a cause, helping a friend in need, or contributing to missions.

Be generous with your time and talents: Generosity is not just about money. Offer your time, skills, and energy to serve others, knowing that these contributions are equally valuable in God's eyes.

Trust in God's provision: As you give generously, trust that God will provide for all your needs. Remember that when we give, it will be given to us, pressed down, shaken together, and running over (Luke 6:38).

Cultivate gratitude: A generous spirit stems from a grateful heart. Regularly reflect on God's blessings, and let that gratitude fuel your desire to give.

Give cheerfully: Knowing that your generosity pleases God. Avoid giving out of guilt or compulsion.

Focus on the intention of your heart when giving rather than the exact percentage.

Approach tithing with a joyful heart, as it is an opportunity to give back to God through worship and gratitude.

Make generosity a lifestyle: Integrating giving into your daily life makes it a habit that reflects your faith and trust in God. Let generosity become a natural part of who you are.

Why Must You Tithes

According to naturalistic theories, giving is deeply ingrained in our biology, psychology, and social structures. The benefits of nurturing generosity—such as strengthened social bonds, improved mental and physical well-being, and increased social capital—are substantial and far outweigh any potential drawbacks. In contrast, lacking generosity can result in isolation, stress, and weaker social connections, hurting overall well-being. By embracing giving and integrating it into our lives, we not only enhance the lives of others but also experience significant benefits for ourselves. Generosity goes beyond being a moral or ethical choice; it serves as a pathway to a healthier, happier, and more interconnected life.

- Tithing is a discipline that enables believers to trust in God's provision. By allocating a portion of our income to God, we are reminded that He is our provider and that we can depend on Him to meet our needs.

- Tithing is a practice that strengthens our faith and helps us focus on God rather than material possessions. For those new to tithing, it is recommended that they start with a manageable percentage and gradually increase it as their trust in God grows. The key is to begin and trust God with our resources.

- Tithing helps believers grow in faith and trust that God will provide them.

- Tithing encourages us to go beyond tithing and live a life of generosity by giving our time, talents, and resources whenever and wherever they are needed.

- Tithing helps believers cultivate a generous heart, but it should be paired with a willingness to give sacrificially and spontaneously, as God leads.

- Tithing is a starting point for a lifestyle of generosity.

- Be open to giving beyond the tithe and respond to needs around you and God's prompting.

- Generosity extends beyond finances to include time, talents, and love.

- Use all you must serve others and advance God's kingdom.

- Approach tithing with grace and not legalism, as God cares more about the condition of your heart than rigid adherence to rules.

- Tithing should be done out of a genuine desire to worship God and support His work, not out of guilt or compulsion.

- Tithing should be motivated by love and faith, not a sense of obligation, and should be an expression of joy and trust.

- Increased Social Status and Reputation: Generosity can enhance an individual's social status and reputation, making them more respected and valued within their community. This can lead to increased social support and opportunities.

Reciprocal Benefits: Engaging in acts of giving often leads to reciprocity, where others are more likely to help or support you in return. This can provide tangible benefits, such as assistance during difficult times.

Increased Happiness and Well-Being: Generosity correlates with heightened happiness and life-satisfying action. The activation of the brain's reward system provides immediate emotional benefits, making giving a fulfilling and rewarding experience.

Stress Reduction: Acts of giving, especially those involving social connection and why, have been proven to lower stress levels. The release of oxytocin and other positive neurochemicals can counteract the effects of stress and promote "a sense of calm and well-being.

The Tithe Dilemma

Improved Physical Health: Regular acts of giving have been associated with improved physical health, including lower blood pressure, a more robust immune" system, and a longer lifespan. These health benefits are likely linked to the reduction in stress and the positive emotional states associated with giving.

Strengthened Social Relationships: Giving fosters a sense of mutual obligation and trust within relationships, leading to more robust and more stable social connections. These relationships can provide emotional support, companionship, and practical assistance.

Cultivating Social Capital: When individuals give and help others, they build social capital – a valuable network of relationships and goodwill that can be relied upon in times of need. This social capital is beneficial for personal and professional success.

Emotional Satisfaction: Acts of giving, mainly when acknowledged, or rent an individual in the sense of satisfaction and fulfillment. This emotional gratification reinforces the behavior and promotes continued generosity.

Sustained Survival and Achievement: Over time, individuals and groups practicing generosity and cooperation are more likely to thrive than those not. The advantages of social support, mutual assistance, and strengthened social bonds far outweigh the potential short-term costs of giving.

Positive Reinforcement Cycle: Generosity initiates a positive reinforcement cycle where giving leads to reciprocal benefits, encouraging further generosity. This cycle fortifies the social structure and improves the community's overall well-being.

200 | P a g e

Enhanced Mental and Physical Health: Giving has been shown to have significant psychological benefits, including increased happiness and reduced stress, contributing to overall mental well-being. Conversely, a lack of generosity may lead to feelings of isolation, decreased social support, and higher stress and anxiety levels. Additionally, giving has been associated with improved cardiovascular health and longevity, suggesting far-reaching positive effects on physical well-being that are not typically associated with a non-generous lifestyle.

Sustained and Fulfilling Relationships: Generosity and mutual support are critical to long-lasting and fulfilling relationships. Conversely, relationships where individuals focus only on receiving or minimizing their giving are often less stable and less satisfying.

Reciprocity, Trust, and Social Cohesion: Generosity fosters a culture of reciprocity and trust, enhancing social cohesion and cooperation. These benefits contribute to a more supportive and resilient community, which benefits everyone involved.

Benefit of Tithing and Giving

Enhanced Social Bonds: Giving strengthens relationships and fosters a sense of community trust and cooperation, leading to a more cohesive and supportive social network, which is beneficial for individual well-being and group survival.

Increased Social Status and Reputation: Generosity can enhance an individual's social status and reputation, earning them more respect and value within their community and increasing social support and opportunities.

Reciprocal Benefits: Acts of giving often lead to reciprocity, with others more likely to help or support you in return, providing tangible benefits such as assistance during difficult times.

The Long-Term Benefits of Generosity and Cooperation: Over time, individuals and groups prioritizing generosity and cooperation are more likely to experience long-term success and well-being than those not. The advantages of social support, mutual aid, and strengthened social bonds far outweigh any short-term costs associated with giving.

Creating a Positive Feedback Loop: Generosity initiates a positive feedback loop where giving results in reciprocal benefits, further motivating individuals to continue being generous. This feedback loop contributes to the strengthening of social connections and the overall enhancement of community well-being.

Neuroscientific findings have revealed that acts of giving activate the brain's reward system, particularly areas associated with pleasure and satisfaction, such as the ventral striatum. When individuals engage in meaningful and selfless giving, they often experience a "helper's high" – a sense of euphoria and deep satisfaction.

Oxytocin, often called the "love hormone," is vital in fostering social bonds and has been associated with fostering feelings of trust, empathy, and generosity. Engaging in acts of giving can trigger the release of oxytocin, strengthening the connection between the giver and the recipient.

Enhanced Happiness and Well-Being: Giving increases happiness and overall life satisfaction. Activating the brain's reward system brings immediate emotional benefits, making generosity a profoundly fulfilling and rewarding experience.

Stress Reduction: Acts of giving, particularly those involving social connection and empathy, have been proven to lower stress levels. The release of oxytocin and other positive neurochemicals can counteract the effects of stress and promote a feeling of tranquility and well-being.

Improved Physical Health: Regular acts of giving have been associated with better physical health, including lower blood pressure, a more robust immune system, and a longer lifespan. These health benefits are likely linked to the reduction in stress and the positive emotional states associated with giving.

Enhanced Mental Health: The psychological benefits of giving, such as increased happiness and reduced stress, contribute to overall mental well-being. Conversely, a lack of generosity may lead to feelings of isolation, decreased social support, and higher stress and anxiety levels.

Physical Health Benefits: The physical health advantages associated with giving, such as improved cardiovascular health and longevity, suggest that giving has extensive positive effects on the body. These benefits are typically not associated with a non-generous lifestyle.

Strengthened Social Relationships: Giving fosters mutual obligation and trust within relationships, resulting in more robust and more enduring social connections. These relationships can offer emotional support, companionship, and practical assistance.

Enhanced Social Capital: By giving and helping others, individuals cultivate social capital—a network of relationships and goodwill that can be relied upon in times of need. This social capital is beneficial for both personal and professional success.

Emotional Fulfillment: Giving brings fulfillment and satisfaction, especially when appreciated or reciprocated. This emotional reward reinforces the behavior and motivates continued generosity.

Sustained Relationships: Relationships characterized by generosity and mutual support are more likely to be long-lasting and fulfilling. In contrast, relationships where individuals focus only on receiving or minimizing their giving are often less stable and less satisfying.

Generosity fosters a culture of reciprocity and trust, enhancing social cohesion and cooperation. These positive outcomes create a more supportive and resilient community, benefiting everyone involved.

According to naturalistic theories, giving is deeply ingrained in our biology, psychology, and social structures. The benefits of generosity, such as strengthened social bonds, improved mental and physical health, and increased social capital, far outweigh potential costs. Conversely, lacking generosity can lead to isolation, stress, and weaker social connections, harming overall well-being.

Tithing is an act of worship that acknowledges God as the source of all blessings. By giving back a portion of what God has provided, believers recognize that everything they have belongs to God and that He is the ultimate provider.

In the Old Testament, tithing was used to sustain the Levites, who were entrusted with Israel's religious and ceremonial obligations. This concept carries over to the New Testament, where followers are urged to support those who spread and teach the gospel.

Tithing also cared for the less fortunate, including people experiencing poverty, orphans, widows, and foreigners. This reflects God's commitment to justice and compassion for the marginalized. *Tithing* is a practice that fosters discipline and faith in the life of a believer. It necessitates trust in God's provision and helps believers prioritize God in their financial affairs.

Some Christians believe that although tithing is a commendable practice, it is not mandatory under the New Covenant. They stress that giving should stem from grace rather than obligation and that the New Testament promotes generosity without specifying a specific percentage.

Tithing also serves as an act of obedience to God's commands. Even in challenging times, giving back to God reflects a dedication to following His guidance.

Tithing nurtures a sense of community as believers contribute to the common good. It ensures the sustainability of the church and its ministries and supports the less fortunate.

Final Note and Encouragement

The Tithe Dilemma: Exploring the Blessings and Challenges of Giving in Faith. Exploring the biblical foundations, Jesus' teachings, and the early church's practices has enriched your understanding of giving. More importantly, I hope it has ignited in you a desire to live generously, not out of duty, but from a heart transformed by God's grace.

Tithing and giving are not merely financial decisions but acts of worship, trust, and obedience. They mirror the condition of our hearts and our readiness to join God in His work on earth. Scripture reminds us that giving is more than a transaction—it is a compelling declaration of our faith in God's provision and a tangible way to demonstrate His love to the world.

For some, tithing may still seem daunting, particularly in financial uncertainty. Nevertheless, I urge you to start from where you are. Keep in mind that God sees the heart, not the amount. Begin with what you can give and trust Him to nurture your faith and expand your capacity to give as you continue on this journey.

Generosity is more than just a one-time act or a specific percentage. It is a way of life that encompasses how we interact with others and use the time, talents, and resources entrusted to us. It is about blessing others and contributing to the growth of God's kingdom. Embracing this lifestyle will reveal that giving is more fulfilling than receiving.

I encourage you to continue growing in generosity. Let your giving flow from the grace and love you have received from God. Trust Him at every stage of your journey, knowing that He will meet your needs and use your generosity to impact others' lives and advance His kingdom.

May you find joy, freedom, and blessings in living a life of giving. Moreover, may your generosity reflect the selflessness of the One who gave everything for us.

Blessings,

Najeem Atinsola

Author

Case Studies

Tithe and Offering with Biblical Resolutions

Tithing and offering practices often pose real-world challenges and dilemmas for Christians. These case studies highlight some of the practical challenges believers face when it comes to tithing and offering. Each scenario is unique, but biblical principles offer clear guidance on navigating these issues in a way that honors God, promotes generosity, and fosters spiritual growth. By seeking God's wisdom and aligning with Scripture, Christians can resolve these dilemmas with faith, trust, and a cheerful heart for giving, finding relief and peace in their decisions.

Case Study 1: Tithing While in Debt

Dilemma: John, a local church member, has always been committed to tithing. However, he is struggling to continue this practice due to recent financial challenges and credit card debt. His income barely covers his expenses, leaving him wanting to decide whether to prioritize paying off his debt or continuing to tithe, even if it means further financial strain.

Resolution

John should consider two critical biblical principles. Firstly, the Bible encourages believers to be wise stewards of their finances. Proverbs 22:7 states, 'The rich rule over the poor, and the borrower is slave to the lender,' emphasizing the importance of managing and avoiding debt. This principle instills a sense of responsibility and empowerment in John, guiding him to make wise financial decisions.

At the same time, 2 Corinthians 8:12 provides guidance on giving: 'For if the willingness is there, the gift is acceptable according to what one has, not according to what one does not have.' John is encouraged to live according to his current ability, even if it is not the traditional 10%. He can contribute a smaller portion while working toward paying off his debt, trusting that God sees his willingness and desire to give. As his financial situation improves, he can gradually increase his giving, knowing that his giving, no matter the amount, is practical and pleasing to God.

Case Study 2: Should I Give to My Church or a Charity?

Dilemma: Mary finds herself torn between tithing to her church, which relies on regular offerings, and supporting a nonprofit organization that provides clean water to needy communities.

Resolution: The Bible stresses the significance of supporting the local church, as evidenced in Malachi 3:10, which urges believers to "Bring the whole tithe into the storehouse, that there may be food in my house." The "storehouse" is often interpreted as the local church, where spiritual nourishment is provided, and ministry is carried out. Additionally, 1 Corinthians 9:14 reminds believers that "the Lord has commanded that those who preach the gospel should receive their living from it."

Nevertheless, the Bible also encourages believers to be generous beyond the church. Galatians 6:10 states, "Therefore, as we have opportunity, let us do good to all people, especially those who belong to the family of believers." This implies that while the local church should be a priority, believers are encouraged to support other causes and ministries.

A balanced approach for Mary is crucial. It might involve continuing to tithe to her church as her primary place of giving while also setting aside additional offerings or donations for the charity she is passionate about. This approach would honor her church's needs while contributing to God's work.

Case Study 3: Transparency and Misuse of Church Funds
Scenario:

Tom and Lisa have faithfully tithed to their church for years. Recently, rumors have surfaced about the potential misuse of funds by the church leadership, with concerns that more money is being spent on building renovations rather than outreach and missions. Tom and Lisa are now uncertain about continuing their tithing if they are unsure about the proper use of their contributions.

Resolution:

Transparency and accountability in tithes and offerings are crucial, as churches are called to steward resources wisely. 1 Timothy 3:2 highlights the need for church leaders to "be "above reproach" in their conduct, including financial matters. Churches should establish systems of accountability to ensure that funds are appropriately utilized for ministry, outreach, and aiding the needy.

While it is valid for Tom and Lisa to raise concerns, the Bible also instructs believers to continue giving in faith, trusting God rather than focusing solely on human imperfections. In 2 Corinthians 8:20-21, Paul emphasizes transparency in financial matters, stating, "We want to avoid any criticism of the way we administer this significant gift. For we are taking pains to do what is right, not only in the eyes of the Lord bu" also in the eyes of man."

Tom and Lisa can respectfully approach church leadership to inquire about fund management. If the leadership is open and transparent, they can be reassured that their tithes are being used effectively. However, if there is ongoing financial mismanagement, it might be time to consider alternative giving avenues while remaining committed to generosity prayerfully.

Case Study 4: Giving Out of Guilt or Obligation

Sarah has been feeling pressured by her church to give more. During services, the offering is repeatedly emphasized, and there are appeals for special donations almost weekly. Sarah feels guilty for not being able to give more and wonders if her giving is genuinely pleasing to God if it is done out of obligation rather than joy.

Resolution:

The Bible emphasizes that giving should be done willingly and cheerfully, not out of guilt or compulsion. 2 Corinthians 9:7 says, "Each of you should give what has" decided in your heart to give, not reluctantly or under compulsion, for God loves a cheerful giver." This verse underscores that Go values are the heart behind giving more than the amount.

Sarah should not feel pressured to give beyond her means or capacity. Giving should flow from gratitude and a desire to honor God, not from fear or obligation. She can prayerfully decide what she can give, keeping her heart aligned with God's desire for joyful and willing God. Suppose the church's emphasis on giving is the cause of church's pressure. In that case, it might be helpful for Sarah to have an honest conversation with church leadership about how the offering is presented during services.

Case Study 5: Tithing During Retirement

Scenario:

James and Margaret, now retired and living on a fixed income, are still determining how much they should tithe, given their reduced financial resources. Despite faithfully tithing during their working years, they feel constrained by their new financial reality and are still determining the appropriate amount to give.

Resolution:

The principle of tithing is not solely about adhering to a specific percentage but rather about giving in proportion to what God has provided. As 2 Corinthians 8: "2 states, "For if the willingness is there, the gift is acceptable according to what one has, not according to what one does" not have." This suggests that God understands when circumstances change and values a willing heart regardless of the amount.

James and Margaret can continue to give based on their current financial situation, even if it is less than what they gave during their working years. What matters most is their faithfulness and desire to honor God with what they have. Additionally, they can contribute through acts of service and volunteering, using their time and talents to give in other ways beyond financial offerings.

Case Study 6: **Can I Stop Tithing to Save for a Major Purchase?**

Scenario:

David and his wife are saving for a down payment on their first home. With the rising cost of housing, they need to direct all their extra funds toward savings. David wonders if it would be okay to pause tithing for a year until they reach their financial goal.

Resolution:

While the desire to save for a home is understandable, the Bible encourages believers to trust God with their finances and to give even in times of financial planning or constraint. Pr" verbs 3:9-10 says, "Honor the Lord with your wealth, with the first fruits of all your crops; then your barns will be filled to overflowing, and your vats will brim" over with new wine." This principle of giving the first portion to God reflects trust in His provision.

David should consider continuing to give, even if it is at a reduced level while working toward his financial goal. Tithing is an act of faith, and God promises to bless those who honor Him with their resources. David can prayerfully ask God for wisdom in balancing his savings plan with his desire to remain faithful in giving.

Faith Questions About Tithing in the Church Today

Tithing and offering practices often present real-world challenges and dilemmas for Christians. These case studies highlight some practical challenges believers face regarding tithing and offering. Each scenario is unique, but biblical principles offer clear guidance on navigating these issues in a way that honors God, promotes generosity, and fosters spiritual growth. By seeking God's wisdom and aligning with Scripture, Christians can resolve these dilemmas with faith, trust, and a cheerful heart for giving, finding relief and peace in their decisions.

Tithing remains a significant topic within Christian communities, sparking various questions about its relevance, practice, and purpose in the modern Church. Below are some of the most common faith questions related to tithing and biblical insights to provide clarity and guidance.

Is tithing still required for Christians today?

Question:

Is tithing still considered a requirement in the New Testament, or is it an Old Testament practice no longer relevant under the New Covenant?

Answer:

Tithing originates from Old Testament law as a command to give 10% (Leviticus 27:30, Numbers 18:21). However, the New Testament emphasizes generosity and a heart of giving. While Jesus did not explicitly abolish tithing, he emphasized that faithful giving goes beyond legalism. In Matthew 23:23, Jesus criticized the Pharisees for prioritizing tithing over justice, mercy, and faithfulness, suggesting that tithing is valuable but incomplete without a transformed heart.

Paul stresses generosity based on what one has, not out of compulsion but cheerfully, in 2 Corinthians 9:7: "Each of you should give what you have decided in your heart to give, not reluctantly or under compulsion, for God loves a cheerful giver." The New Testament encourages believers to give generously as an act of faith and worship, making the principle of tithing still relevant but with a focus on the heart rather than strict percentages.

Does tithing only refer to money, or can I tithe my time and talents?

Question:

Can tithing be about giving time and talents, or does it strictly refer to monetary giving?

Answer:

The Bible emphasizes the importance of financial giving as part of tithing (Malachi 3:10), but it also encourages believers to give of their whole selves, including time, talents, and resources. In Romans 12:1, Paul writes, "Offer your bodies as a living sacrifice, holy and pleasing to God—this is your true and proper worship." This indicates that all of who we are—our talents, time, and abilities—can be offered to God in service.

Moreover, 1 Peter 4:10 encourages believers to use their gifts to serve others: "Each of you should use whatever gift you have received to serve others, as faithful stewards of God's grace in its various forms." While financial giving remains important, God also calls us to give of our time and talents, making service and generosity a holistic practice.

What if I cannot afford to tithe?

Question:

How can I tithe when facing financial difficulties and barely meeting my needs?

Answer:

The story of the widow's offering in Mark 12:41-44 serves as a potent reminder that God values the heart behind our giving more than the amount. Despite giving only two small coins, all she had, Jesus commended the widow's sacrificial gift. In 2 Corinthians 8:12, Paul also emphasizes giving according to what we have, not what we do not have. If you face financial challenges, start with what you can give, knowing God sees and honors your faithfulness.

Where should my tithe go? Should I give it to the Church or donate it to other causes?

Question:

Is my tithe only supposed to go to my local Church, or can I direct it toward other ministries and charitable causes?

Answer:

The biblical basis for tithing primarily involves supporting the work of the local Church or religious community. In Malachi 3:10, God instructs, "Bring the whole tithe into the storehouse, that there may be food in my house." The "storehouse" is often understood as the temple in the Old Testament context, but it is interpreted today as the local Church, which plays a vital role in ministry and spreading the gospel.

However, the New Testament emphasizes broader generosity beyond the local Church. Galatians 6:10 encourages believers to "do good to all people, especially those who belong to the family of believers." This suggests that while tithing to your Church is essential, giving beyond that to support other ministries, missions, and those in need is also a biblical principle.

What is the difference between tithes and offerings?

Question

What is the distinction between tithing and giving offerings? Are they the same thing?

Answer

Tithing involves giving a specific portion, traditionally 10%, of one's income as directed in the Old Testament (Leviticus 27:30). Offerings, on the other hand, are voluntary contributions that exceed the tithe and are often given out of gratitude or in response to a particular need.

In 2 Corinthians 9:7, Paul addresses the concept of offerings, stating, "Each of you should give what you have decided in your heart to give, not reluctantly or under compulsion, for God loves a cheerful giver." Offerings exemplify a spirit of generosity that transcends obligation, showcasing a deeper form of giving rooted in love and faith.

Does God promise blessings for those who tithe?

Question:

Is it biblical to expect blessings in return for tithing, or is this a misunderstanding?

Answer

In Malachi 3:10-12, God promises to bless those who faithfully tithe: "Bring the whole tithe into the storehouse… Test me in this… and see if I will not throw open the floodgates of heaven and pour out so much blessing that there will not be room enough to store it." This passage emphasizes that God does promise to bless those who give generously, although the blessings may not always be material.

However, in the New Testament, the focus shifts toward giving without expectation. Luke 6:38 says, "Give, and it will be given to you… For with the measure you use, it will be measured to you." While blessings may come, the emphasis is on giving from a place of love and faith, not out of a desire to receive. God's blessings may come in many forms—spiritual growth, joy, contentment, or strengthened relationships—not just financial gain.

Should I tithe on my gross or net income?

Question

Should tithing be based on gross income (before taxes) or net income (after taxes)?

Answer:

The Bible does not specify whether tithing should be calculated on gross or net income. However, the fundamental principle of giving your "first fruits" remains crucial. Proverbs 3:9 advises, "Honor the Lord with your wealth, with the first fruits of all your crops." First fruits symbolize the best and initial portion of what you receive, signifying confidence in God's provision before anything else.

Many believers tithe based on gross income to honor God with the first and best of their earnings. Nevertheless, the most significant factor is the attitude of the heart. Whether you tithe on gross or net income, the essential thing is to give generously and faithfully, relying on God's provision.

Is Tithing a New Testament Requirement?

Controversy

Some argue that tithing is an Old Testament law no longer required for Christians living under the New Covenant. They believe that since Jesus fulfilled the law, tithing as a legal requirement is obsolete.

Answer

Tithing has roots in the Old Testament (Leviticus 27:30, Malachi 3:10), but the New Testament emphasizes the spirit of giving rather than a strict legal obligation. In Matthew 23:23, Jesus discusses tithing and criticizes the Pharisees for their legalistic approach, highlighting the importance of justice, mercy, and faithfulness in addition to tithing. While not dismissing tithing, Jesus underscores the significance of giving from a transformed heart.

Furthermore, 2 Corinthians 9:7 encourages cheerful and voluntary giving: "Each of you should give what you have decided in your heart to give, not reluctantly or under compulsion, for God loves a cheerful giver." Although the New Testament does not mandate the exact practice of tithing (10%), the principle of generous, faith-driven giving remains a consistent biblical teaching.

Should Tithes Only Be Given to the Church?

Controversy

Many churches teach that tithes should only be given to the local Church, but some believe that tithes can be directed toward other ministries, charitable causes, or individuals in need. This leads to the question: Is the local Church the sole recipient of the tithe?

Biblical Answer

In the Old Testament, tithes were brought into the "storehouse" (the temple) to support the Levites, priests, and temple work (Malachi 3:10). This principle of supporting those who do the work of ministry is echoed in the New Testament. 1 Corinthians 9:13-14 states: "Don't you know that those who serve in the temple get their food from the temple, and those who serve at the altar share what is offered on the altar? In the same way, the Lord has commanded that those who preach the gospel should receive their living from the gospel."

While the New Testament encourages supporting the local Church, it also strongly emphasizes broader generosity. Galatians 6:10

encourages believers to "do good to all people, especially those who belong to the family of believers." Giving to other causes, ministries, or individuals in need is also biblical, if it is done with the heart of advancing God's kingdom and helping others.

Is Tithing a "Prosperity Gospel" Practice?

Controversy

The "Prosperity Gospel" teaches that if you give, primarily through tithing, God will bless you financially. Some preachers promise material wealth and success in exchange for tithing, which has led to suspicion and skepticism about tithing in general. Many people feel manipulated or coerced into giving.

Biblical Answer

While the Bible promises blessings for those who give generously (see Malachi 3:10 and Luke 6:38), it does not support giving as a guaranteed formula for financial gain. The blessings associated with tithing and giving are often spiritual, relational, or in terms of increased faith and contentment, not necessarily material wealth.

In 1 Timothy 6:6-10, Paul warns against pursuing wealth: "For the love of money is a root of all kinds of evil. Some people, eager for money, have wandered from the faith and pierced themselves with many griefs." Tithing is about trusting God and investing in His kingdom, not securing personal financial prosperity. Believers should give with the motivation to honor God, not to "buy" blessings.

Should People Tithe When They Are in Debt or Financial Strain?

Controversy

Another contention is whether Christians should tithe when they are in debt or facing financial hardship. Some argue that people should prioritize paying off debts or providing for their families, while others maintain that tithing should remain a priority, even in financial difficulty.

Biblical Answer

The Bible teaches us to give according to what we have, not what we lack. 2 Corinthians 8:12 says, "For if the willingness is there, the gift is acceptable according to what one has, not according to what one does not have." This indicates that God does not expect us to give beyond our means.

However, giving during financial hardship can demonstrate a profound act of faith. For instance, Jesus praised the widow in Mark 12:41-44 for giving out of her poverty rather than out of abundance. The key is to seek God's wisdom and discernment. A balanced approach is wise if tithing leads to neglecting basic needs or worsening financial distress. Give what you can, and trust God with your finances while working to improve your situation.

How Should the Church use tithes and Offerings?

Controversy:

Congregations often debate how churches should spend the tithes and offerings they receive. Should the funds be used primarily for church operations (e.g., staff salaries, building maintenance), or should more be directed toward missions, outreach, and helping the poor?

Biblical Answer:

The Bible offers guidance on supporting church leaders and aiding the less fortunate. According to 1 Timothy 5:17-18, it is essential to provide financial support for church leaders who lead well, particularly those dedicated to preaching and teaching. Likewise, 1 Corinthians 9:14 reinforces this by asserting that those who preach the gospel should receive their living from it.

Simultaneously, Scripture underscores the significance of caring for the impoverished and those in need. James 1:27 teaches that true religion, in God's eyes, involves looking after orphans and widows in their distress. Churches are thus called to strike a balance in the allocation of funds, supporting ministry efforts while meeting the community's needs.

Ultimately, churches are encouraged to be transparent in their use of funds and to ensure that resources are managed to reflect God's compassion for His people and the broader world.

Is There Pressure to Give in Modern Churches?

Controversy:

Some people feel pressured or manipulated into giving, particularly in churches that emphasizing tithing or offerings during worship. This can lead to resentment or reluctance, as people may feel they are giving out of compulsion rather than from a willing heart.

Biblical Answer

It is important to remember that the Bible emphasizes that giving should always be voluntary and joyful. 2 Corinthians 9:7 states, "Each of you should give what you have decided in your heart to give, not reluctantly or under compulsion, for God loves a cheerful giver." Therefore, churches should prioritize teaching the biblical principles of generosity and trust in God's provision while allowing members to give willingly and joyfully.

Using pressure tactics can diminish the spiritual significance of giving, which is intended to be an act of worship. Leaders should promote giving as an opportunity for members to invest in God's kingdom and participate in His work rather than as a burdensome duty.

Further Reading and References

1. The Holy Bible, New International Version (NIV).

Biblical references throughout the book, including passages on tithing, generosity, and giving, are taken from the NIV.

- Genesis 14:18-20: Abram gives a tenth to Melchizedek.
- Genesis 28:20-22: Jacob vows to give a tenth to God.
- Leviticus 27:30-32: The tithe is holy and belongs to the Lord.
- Numbers 18:21-24: The tithe supports the Levites.
- Deuteronomy 14:22-2": Instructions on tithing and care for the needy.
- Malachi 3:8-12: God's call to faithfulness in tithing.
- Matthew 23:23: Jesus criticizes the Pharisees for their legalistic tithing.
- Hebrews 7:1-10: Abraham's tithe to Melchizedek.
- 2 Corinthians 9:6-7: The principle of cheerful giving."

Alnehabi, M., & Alnehabi, M. (2023). The Association between Corporate Social Responsibility, Employee Performance, and Turnover Intention Moderated by Organizational Identification and Commitment. Sustainability, 15(19), 14202.

Gbadamosi, A. Q. An Internet of Things enabled system for real-time monitoring and predictive maintenance of railway infrastructure. https://core.ac.uk/download/590243048.pdf

Blomberg, Craig L. Neither Poverty Nor Riches: A Biblical Theology of Possessions. IVP Academic, 2000. *This work explores the biblical perspective on wealth and possessions, offering insight into the theology of giving and financial stewardship.*

Keller, Timothy. Generous Justice: How God's Grace Makes Us Just. Riverhead Books, 2012. *Keller's work connects justice and generosity, showing how Christians are called to live out God's grace through acts of generosity and compassion.*

Stott, John R.W. The Message of the Sermon on the Mount. IVP Academic, 1993. *In this study of Jesus' Sermon on the Mount, Stott delves into the heart of Christian living, including principles of giving and selflessness.*

Sider, Ronald J. Rich Christians in an Age of Hunger: Moving from Affluence to Generosity. Thomas Nelson, 2005. *Sider addresses the moral implications of wealth and poverty in the world, encouraging Christians to live generously and address global injustice.*

Barna, George. Revolutionary Generosity: How Giving Transforms Us, Our Church, and Our World. Barna Group, 2006. *Barna's book discusses the transformational power of generosity within the individual believer, the church, and the world.*

Wright, N.T. Simply Christian: Why Christianity Makes Sense. HarperOne, 2006. *Wright touches on the Christian life and how believers are called to live out their faith in generosity, reflecting God's justice and mercy.*

McKnight, Scot. The King Jesus Gospel: The Original Good News Revisited. Zondervan, 2011. *McKnight provides insight into the gospel's call for a life of generosity, highlighting the importance of living out kingdom values.*

Foster, Richard J. Celebration of Discipline: The Path to Spiritual Growth. HarperCollins, 1998. *Foster's classic work on spiritual disciplines includes a chapter on simplicity and stewardship, emphasizing the importance of giving as a spiritual practice.*

Powell, Mark Allan. Giving to God: The Bible's Good News About Living a Generous Life. Wm. B. Eerdmans Publishing Co., 2006. *Powell explores the biblical principles of giving, emphasizing the joy and freedom of living generously.*

Colophon

The book was meticulously crafted to prioritize clarity, scriptural integrity, and accessibility. Its purpose is to guide believers as they explore the principles of tithing, generosity, and faithful stewardship.

Typography

The body text is presented in Garamond, carefully chosen for its readability and elegance. This makes the content inviting and easy to follow. Chapter titles and headings also use Garamond, ensuring a clear and consistent hierarchy for navigating the book.

Design and Layout

The book's layout balances aesthetics and functionality to ensure readers can easily engage with the content. Consideration was given to white space, line spacing, and font sizes to promote a comfortable reading experience. Additionally, visual elements have been strategically incorporated to enhance the clarity of key concepts and provide visual breaks between sections.

Production

This book has been printed by [Printer/Publisher] using environmentally responsible methods, demonstrating a commitment to stewardship in its content and production.

Scripture References

Unless otherwise noted, all Scripture references are from New International Version [NIV] to ensure consistency and clarity for readers from diverse denominational backgrounds.

We trust this book will encourage believers to live out their faith with God's confidence in God's provision. May it serve as a valuable resource for years to come.

Published by

Authentic Spiritual Values Group
Texas, USA
2024

Made in the USA
Columbia, SC
14 December 2024

48175951R00126